BEFORE YOU LOSE YOUR MIND

DECONSTRUCTING BAD THEOLOGY IN THE CHURCH

EDITED BY KEITH GILES

BRANDON ANDRESS · MICHELLE COLLINS · DERRICK DAY
MATTHEW J. DISTEFANO · BRANDON DRAGAN · JASON ELAM
MARIA FRANCESCA FRENCH · MARK GREGORY KARRIS
MATTHEW J. KORPMAN · JOSH ROGGIE
REV. DR. KATY VALENTINE · AND SKEETER WILSON

First Edition

Scripture quotations marked NRSV are taken from the New Revised Standard Version of the Bible, copyright © 1989 by the National Council of the Churches of Christ in the U.S.A. Used by permission. All rights reserved. Scripture quotations marked NIV are from the Holy Bible, New International Version®, NIV®. Copyright © 1973, 1978, 1984, 2011 by Biblica, Inc.™ Used by permission of Zondervan. All rights reserved worldwide. www.zondervan.com. Scripture quotations marked KJV are from the King James Version of the Bible. Scripture quotations marked NLT are from the New Living Translation Version of the Bible, Holy Bible: New Living Translation. Wheaton, IL: Tyndale House Publishers, 2004. Print.

ISBN 978-1-938480-83-6

This volume is printed on acid free paper and meets ANSI Z39.48 standards.

Printed in the United States of America

Published by Quoir
Oak Glen, California
www.quoir.com

CONTENTS

INTRODUCTION

KEITH GILES

"In the case of fundamentalist beliefs, people expect that choosing to leave a childhood faith is like giving up Santa Claus—a little sad, but basically a matter of "growing up. But religious indoctrination can be hugely damaging, and making the break from an authoritarian kind of religion can definitely be traumatic. It involves a complete upheaval of a person's construction of reality, including the self, other people, life, the future, everything. People unfamiliar with it, including therapists, have trouble appreciating the sheer terror it can create and the recovery needed."
– Marlene Winell, PhD

There are a lot of people who are deconstructing their faith today. Some are high-profile Christian theologians, authors, artists, musicians and pastors like Joshua Harris, Derek Webb, David Bazan, Bart Ehrman, Michael Gungor and several others.

But outside of those minor religious celebrities who have experienced this painful process of unraveling their faith in God and Christ, there are probably hundreds of thousands of average

Christians who are quietly, but nevertheless completely undergoing the total deconstruction of their Christianity.

I know what that's like. I've been undergoing my own deconstruction process for about 15 years now. For me, it started with the realization that the Gospel I grew up with wasn't the actual Gospel that Jesus taught. Instead of saying a prayer so I could go to heaven when I die, the Gospel that Jesus proclaimed was all about entering the actual presence of God right here and right now—not sometime after this life was over.

Once that reality sunk in, everything else started to come apart at the seams for me. Next was evangelism, then came the modern version of what Church was supposed to look like, then came the need to focus more on serving people in need rather than grow a large mega-church and put butts in the seats.

From there I began to deconstruct my views about Hell, the Cross, Salvation, the End Times, Homosexuality and even how to think about the Bible.

I wrote blog articles about my doubts and published books about my newfound realizations. Along with that came the double-edged sword of agreement—from those who were starting to ask the same questions—and condemnation—from those who felt the need to defend the status quo from boat-rockers like me.

I was called "Heretic", "False Teacher" and a whole lot worse. But those attacks from strangers on the Internet were peanuts compared to the total rejection and dismissal of dear friends, fellow pastors and sometimes even my own family members who just couldn't find it in their hearts to love me as a brother in Christ because I disagreed with them on a particular doctrine or belief. That was the most painful part.

But, I also took comfort from knowing that I was not alone in that either. There were so many others who came to me privately and told me their stories of rejection by pastors, friends and family over differences in theology.

Over the last few years now, I've published a series of books that have helped many people to further deconstruct the toxic entanglements of faith and politics, the worship of the Bible, and the hierarchical power structures of the Church itself.

I've also had the honor of co-hosting a podcast called *The Heretic Happy Hour* which has become sort of a voice for many people who are going thru the deconstruction process. Thanks to our little hour-long show, thousands of people are discovering they are not alone in the universe and that it's ok to ask questions about the faith they were born into.

But here's something I've just recently started to realize: *With all of this focus on "Deconstruction", there is apparently very little attention paid to the need for "Reconstruction."*

For example, some people I know personally have followed their doubts all the way outside the faith. Much like those high-profile Christian "celebrities" I mentioned earlier, they've questioned everything and ended up with nothing to believe in.

And I get it. I really do. There was one point in my own deconstruction process when I nearly lost my faith entirely. In fact, if it wasn't for the kind attention and gentle counseling of my wife, Wendy, I might seriously have gone off the edge of the cliff and never returned.

For many people, there is no one in their life to do that for them. They have no one to process their doubts with and no resources for reconstructing their faith once they've burned it all down.

What really concerns me, honestly, is the emotional damage of deconstruction. As in the quote by Dr. Marlene Winell above, most people don't understand just how traumatic it can be to lose your faith in God, and in the Church, and in the Bible, and for some, even in Jesus.

To make matters much, much worse, there is the added trauma of being shunned by your friends, cut off from your Church community and treated like a heretic by your own family members over differences of belief.

How does anyone survive something like this? I know many times I would look at myself in the mirror and ask myself, "Why can't you just stop asking so many questions?" But, I can't do that. And many people I know can't either. Maybe you can relate?

You see, once you know something, you can't un-know it. Once you've seen something, you cannot un-see it. And so, people like us are left with an impossible choice: To pretend we still believe things we know are not true—for the sake of unity and continued relationships—*or*, we open our mouths and share what we've learned and face the furnace of doubt and the rejection of those we love most of all.

Most of us can't pretend. Not for very long. So, eventually, our truth becomes known. Our views become spoken. And then our character gets questioned and the condemnation begins.

But, what if there was a place people could go to get help and to heal after this painful deconstruction process is through? What if there was some way to help provide tools for *reconstruction* to those who have deconstructed and have no foundation left to stand on? What if someone could take the time to map out the process for healing, and forgiveness, and letting go to both give and receive practical grace?

Those are the questions I've been asking the last few years now. If you're asking similar questions, I've got some good news for you: You're reading the right book.

My fellow contributors and I have been through exactly the same sort of pain you're feeling now. We've had those same doubts. We've asked those same questions. We've looked at ourselves in the mirror and asked why we can't just go along with the status quo like everyone else.

Asking questions is part of what it means to have faith. The opposite of faith is not doubt, it's certainty. So, the fact that you're questioning what you've been told isn't evidence of your lack of faith, it's evidence that you take your faith seriously enough to examine it and to follow the truth wherever it leads you.

When Jesus said that we should "Repent! For the Kingdom of God is near," in his Sermon on the Mount, he wasn't talking about feeling sorry for your sins. That word in our English Bibles translated as "Repent!" is actually the Greek Word *Metanonia* which literally means "Think Differently!" or "Change Your Mind!" So, if you find yourself thinking differently, or asking questions, or changing your mind about the doctrines of Christianity that were handed to you, you're on the right track. In fact, you cannot enter the Kingdom of God without doing this. So, whatever you do, please do not stop asking questions.

If this is where you find yourself today, we've assembled this book just for you. It is our hope that what we've shared in these pages can help you survive this experience. We also hope that this book will help you to realize one of the most important truths of this journey you're on: *You are not alone!*

And perhaps the second most important truth is this: *You're going the right way. Keep asking. Keep questioning. Keep searching.*

Those who ask questions are closer to God than those who think they know all the answers, anyway.

A FEW WORDS FOR THE AMERICAN CHRISTIAN CHURCH

As you may have noticed, some people are starting to Deconstruct their faith. In response, many churches have bullied, belittled and excommunicated those who dare to question the status quo. On the bright side, I have seen a few churches take a more positive stance by hosting events to address the issue of Deconstruction and some even talk about how to help people move on to Reconstruction.

But, regardless of the response, here's what those Churches need to understand: *If you don't change your Church into a safe place to ask questions and even doubt some of your precious doctrines, people will continue to walk away from you.*

Yes, it's great that some churches are taking notice of the fact that people are Deconstructing their faith. Of course, how could they possibly ignore it when hundreds of thousands of Christians are walking away from the Christian Church? The research is overwhelming and church growth experts have been sounding the alarm for the last decade over the numbers of young people leaving the faith and the rise of the "Nones and the Dones" in the American Evangelical Church.

Yes, admitting you have a problem is the first step. But, to really solve the problem, you need to realize what the cause of the problem is and then be willing to make the necessary changes to reverse the trend.

The problem we're facing is this: Christians are questioning their faith. They are Deconstructing their Christian faith and doubting the beliefs that were handed to them as children. As they defy the status quo of Christianity, they are being attacked as heretics, labelled "divisive" and threatened with eternal damnation for asking too many questions.

This is why they are leaving the Church. Plain and simple, they are being asked to leave, or placed in situations where the only sane choice is to walk away to avoid the abuse.

So, my dear American Christian Church, let me urge you to do this one thing if you want to stop the mass exodus of Deconstructing Christians—Embrace those who doubt and allow them to wrestle through their Deconstruction process.

As long as you continue to hold an iron grip on your certainty and refuse to allow people to work through their uncertainty, those people are going to have no other choice but to walk away.

Now, here's what that would look like: Your pastors are going to have to stop insisting that they "know" everything. Your Bible Teachers are going to have to start inviting people to ask honest questions and take those seriously. Your insistence upon having people sign your Statement of Faith before they can become a member, or teach in your schools or Sunday School classrooms or join your staff is going to have to go away.

To be honest, I don't think my appeal is really going to reach the right people. Most of those who are pushing people away are most likely going to continue to do so in the name of "defending the faith" and "standing up for Biblical truth" or whatever.

But, I have to at least try to speak into those places and let people know why they're seeing so many people walk away from the Church. I need to at least attempt to show Church leaders how they can create safe spaces for doubt and stop hurting those who ask questions about their faith.

If nothing else, those people can no longer say, "I didn't know" or "I had no idea" when they wake up one Sunday and walk into an empty church building.

For those who are creating the toxic atmosphere that is driving people away from the Church, let me just say this: One day you're going to realize all the pain you've caused people. We're hoping to build a safe space where even you are welcome and forgiven for driving us away.

Isn't that what Jesus would want?

1

RESEARCH-BASED REASONS WHY FOLKS ARE DECONSTRUCTING THEIR FAITH

MARK GREGORY KARRIS

"Trauma is personal. It does not disappear if it is not validated. When it is ignored or invalidated the silent screams continue internally, heard only by the one held captive. When someone enters the pain and hears the screams, healing can begin."

– Danielle Bernock

No one wakes up and excitedly tells themselves, "Today is the day I want to start unraveling my faith, throwing myself into the throes of social rejection, despair, and one of the most painful seasons of my life." Rather, it's like realizing, halfway through the day, that you have a massive, splitting headache—it just happens. Sure, we could continually deny, suppress, and repress our doubts, troublesome questions, and piercing splinters of toxic beliefs, but the energy it would require simply becomes too costly. The Deconstruction/ Reconstruction (D/R) journey comes at us like a snowball, slowly moving down the hill in a harrowing winter, building and building and finally crashing through our psyche, leaving us completely disoriented.

It's not your fault that your faith is shaken and your core beliefs about God, the church, the Bible, and yourself are shifting. Life happens. Shift happens. Life changes with or without our gracious consent. In every generation people think, "We are the only ones going through this." However, throughout history there have always been deconversions, reconversions, renovations, reformations, and people who have experienced the agonizing dark night of the soul. Yet, at our present time in religious history, some unique dynamics are brewing that are worthy of reflection. Like a check engine light in a car, they may be warning us of deeper issues bubbling beneath the pristine and polished Christian-surface that point to the origin of the D/R journey so prevalent for folks today.

Around six to ten thousand churches die each year.[1] Those are staggering numbers, aren't they? Sadly, a lot of heartbroken pastors, leaders, and congregants are behind those statistics. One of the fastest growing religious trends in America, when it comes to religious polls, is the rise of the "nones." These "no-religion folk" have catapulted from 12 percent in 2003 to 21 percent of all adults

---

1. Thom S. Rainer, "Hope for Dying Churches," January 16, 2018, https://factsandtrends. net/2018/01/16/hope-for-dying-churches/.

in 2017.[2] They were typically raised without a religious upbringing and can identify themselves as atheists, agnostics, or as those who feel pretty neutral about religion. Nearly two-thirds of all young adults, who once were attending church regularly, have dropped out at one time or another.[3] Twenty-seven percent of Americans consider themselves "spiritual but not religious," a category which has increased eight percentage points in the past five years. On top of all of that, a large percentage of Americans, thirty-four percent to be exact, are "dechurched."[4] The dechurched are the "been there, done that, got the t-shirt" folks (we will talk more about them in a minute).

These present-day religious shifts validate what the late Phyllis Tickle emphasized in her book, *The Great Emergence*. According to Tickle, "The Great Emergence" is a radical and much-needed shift, occurring every five hundred years or so, when the church has an epic theological, doctrinal, ecclesial, and spiritual rummage sale.[5] These shifts and statistics are all a part of what Brian McLaren calls *The Great Spiritual Migration*. In a positive and hopeful tone, McLaren opines that spiritual migration is "not *out of* our religions, but out of our cages and ruts, not as jaded ex-members, but as *hopeful pilgrims moving forward in the journey of faith*."[6] Diana Butler Bass, a connoisseur of religious culture and trends, writes, "People

2. See Allison de Jong, "Protestants Decline, More Have No Religion in a Sharply Shifting Religious Landscape," ABC News poll, May 10, 2018, https://abcnews. go.com/Politics/protestants-decline-religion-sharply-shifting-religious-landscape-poll/ story?id=54995663.

3. David Kinnaman and Mark Matlock, *Faith for Exiles: 5 Ways for a New Generation to Follow Jesus in Digital Babylon* (Grand Rapids: Baker Books, 2019), 15.

4. See Barna, "Church Attendance Trends Around the Country," May 26, 2017, https:// www.barna.com/research/church-attendance-trends-around-country/.

5. See Phyllis Tickle, *The Great Emergence: How Christianity Is Changing and Why* (Grand Rapids: Baker Books, 2012).

6. Brian D. McLaren, *The Great Spiritual Migration: How the World's Largest Religion is Seeking a Better Way to Be Christian* (New York: Convergent, 2017), xii.

believe, but they believe differently than they once did. The theological ground is moving; a spiritual revolution is afoot. And there is a gap between that revolution and the institutions of religious faith."[7]

IDENTIFYING THE DECHURCHED

Sociologists Josh Packard and Ashleigh Hope, authors of the book *Church Refugees: Sociologists Reveal Why People Are Done with the Church but Not Their Faith,* performed one hundred in-depth interviews with people who were disengaging with the church. You probably hate labels as much as I do, but see if you can identify with Packard and Hope's brief definition of the "dechurched": "They're done with church. They're tired and fed up with the church. They're dissatisfied with the structure, social message, and politics of the institutional church, and they've decided they and their spiritual lives are better off lived outside of organized religion."[8] From their interviews, Packard and Hope were able to narrow down common themes as part of people's reasoning for distancing themselves from, or leaving, the church:

- They wanted community . . . and got judgment.
- They wanted to affect the life of the church . . . and got bureaucracy.
- They wanted conversation . . . and got doctrine.
- They wanted meaningful engagement with the world . . . and got moral prescription.[9]

Kathy Escobar's *Faith Shift: Finding Your Way Forward When Everything You Believe is Coming Apart* adds a few helpful

7. Diana Butler Bass, *Grounded: Finding God in the World--a Spiritual Revolution* (New York: HarperOne, 2017), 21.

8. Josh Packard and Ashleigh Hope, *Church Refugees: Sociologists Reveal Why People Are Done with the Church but Not Their Faith* (Loveland, Colorado: Group, 2015), 14.

9. Ibid., 28.

subcategories for those disillusioned by church.[10] She describes *spiritual refugees* as "men and women of all ages and backgrounds whose beliefs have shifted, whose certainty is lost, and whose faith expression is now displaced." She describes *church burnouts* as "people who may have given their lives to congregations, ministries, or theological perspectives, but their passion has waned." And her third subcategory, *freedom seekers*, are people who are "tired of feeling stuck and caged by the systems they have lived in. They long for more."

David Kinnaman is the president of the Barna Group, a respected research group that explores the intersection between faith and culture. In his book, *You Lost Me: Why Young Christians Are Leaving Church . . . and Rethinking Faith*, Kinnaman and his colleagues gathered data from hundreds of thousands of interviews from over a period of twenty-seven years. The purpose of their study was to explore people's faith, church experiences, what pushed them away from the church, and what connections to the church they have chosen to keep.

Kinnaman explains his own subcategories he uses to describe the group he calls "the dones."[11] *Nomads* are frustrated and disillusioned with Christianity, but they are not angry and hostile. They have left the church and are ambivalent about faith, yet remain genuinely spiritual. *Prodigals* are angry. They are done with the toxic religious aspects of the Christian faith. Now that they have left, they are free to be their true selves. And then the *exiles* are still in it to win it, or at least in it to make a difference in the church they love. They are also passionate about the world they live in. However, exiles are profoundly disappointed and confused with the lack of loving and creative cultural engagement by many Christians. Here

10. Kathy Escobar, *Faith Shift: Finding Your Way Forward When Everything You Believe Is Coming Apart* (New York: Convergent Books, 2014), 20.

11. David Kinnaman and Aly Hawkins, *You Lost Me: Why Young Christians Are Leaving Church . . . and Rethinking Faith* (Grand Rapids: Baker Books, 2016), 64–65.

are the broad reasons Kinnaman lists for why Christians distance themselves from church (or ditch it altogether):

> *They find the church to be overprotective, stifling creativity and cultural engagement. Shallow with their formulaic slogans, easy platitudes, and proof texting. Anti-science. Repressive—religious rules. Exclusive—they want to find common ground, even if that means glossing over real differences. Doubtless—the church is not a place to express doubts.*[12]

Do any of these labels and descriptions resonate with you? Whether you consider yourself a Done, Spiritual Refugee, Church Burnout, Freedom Seeker, Dechurched, Nomad, Prodigal, Exile— or whatever label or non-label you feel best describes you—the reality is the same: You are going through (or have gone through) a profound shift that has catapulted you into a season of doubt, distressing emotions, anxiety-provoking and painful social realities, and existential and identity concerns.

You are not alone! We are legion! We are many. And, for good reason.

Christians, including church leaders, unfortunately engage in a whole lot of victim blaming. They harshly blame confused, doubting, and hurting Christians, calling them "lost," "heretics," or simply "wayward sinners." Instead of optimistically considering that the large number of people on the deconstructive journey are part of Spirit-inspired events such as *The Great Emergence* or *The Great Spiritual Migration*, they call the mass exodus of dechurched Christians *The Great Apostasy* or *The Great Spiritual Damnation*. Some church leaders blame Satan, false doctrine, a corrupt culture, and the dechurched themselves while neglecting to take a broader and systemic look at themselves, their decisions (and the choices of those who came before them), or other possible causes of the D/R phenomenon.

Here's the deal: You are *not* a bitter, prodigal son or daughter who chose to take all the beautiful things you learned, along with

---

12. Ibid., 92–93.

your rich inheritance of the Christian faith, only to squander it in some big debauched and satanic soirée. Instead, the well of your heart has been poisoned by various elements of current Christian principles, practices, policies, and attitudes.

REASONS FOR DITCHING THE CHURCH

I've compiled my own list of the main reasons people are becoming disenchanted with the church. Based on the qualitative and quantitative data (stories, interviews, assessments, and statistics) compiled by sociologists and psychologists, this list also includes the stories of many people I have personally engaged with as a therapist, friend, or on social media as I listened with compassion.

Politics and Bureaucracy

In the face of church politics and bureaucracy, some people feel they are unable to make a difference in the church. For example, some have powerful gifts to share, but because they're divorced, gay, too young, too old, not attractive enough, not articulate enough, not white enough, not abled enough, not educated enough, or simply female, they are not allowed to uniquely contribute to the life of the church. When bureaucracy or politics play too much of a role in the church, people can often feel left-out and sidelined. They feel as if there is an in-crowd and an out-crowd. They may have tried to start a ministry, or to engage in a particular area of the church, but for reasons they never understood (unless the reasons have been made explicit), it felt like they were perpetually trying to chisel through a thick brick wall. Ultimately, this has led to their disillusionment and feeling as if they don't belong.

Jason was educated, a gifted communicator, and passionate about God and the health of the church. Although he considered the Bible his sacred text, he was not able to teach, preach, or lead any kind of workshops because he held slightly different views on the inspiration of the Scriptures. He stated, "I feel stuck. I feel heartbroken. I feel like there is something wrong with me. The leadership knows my character. They know I love Jesus. They know I have been trained in homiletics and have performed workshops in the community. But why is it that, if I believe slightly different ideas about the formation of the Bible, I am automatically out of the running for using my gifts in the church? It is just sad."

Cora, a 66-year old woman who participated in Packard and Hope's study, had been a Christian for decades. She shared her story about how the church's politics and bureaucracy got in the way of her following the passion God placed in her heart:

> It was fine as long as I was doing what I was told. As long as I was plugged into what someone else had put forth, it was no problem. But when I wanted to do something on my own, it was a whole other story. The last thing I tried to do was start a little group to help the elderly people in our congregation, where we would just go and mow lawns and wash windows and do things for people who needed it. But that never came about. There were so many rules and regulations just to mow lawns that I just backed off of it. It's weird, because we were such a big church you would think this little thing would be easy. But I talked to the missions minister and he told me to come up with a name for my group, propose a budget, write out a mission statement, come to the board hearing and figure out a way to report back every month. I told him, "Really? I just want to mow lawns. Why do we have to do all that?" He told me the board didn't like things going on in the church unless they could oversee it. And here's the kicker, they weren't offering me anything in return. No budget, no help recruiting or organizing. It was just about control. So by that time, I was like "Okay, never mind. I'll just do this on my own."[13]

Since church politics and bureaucracy are overseen mostly by men, there can be strains of misogyny and patriarchy, interlaced with theology, that are oppressive to women and marginalized people. During a recent "Truth Matters Conference," John MacArthur, the posterchild of conservative evangelical Christianity, was asked to give a word association about Beth Moore, a well-known

13. Josh Packard and Todd W. Ferguson, "Being Done: Why People Leave the Church, But Not Their Faith," *Sociological Perspectives* 62, no. 4 (August 2019), 499–517.

female Bible teacher. MacArthur's response was, "Go home." He then proceeded to say, "There is no case that can be made biblically for a woman preacher. Period. Paragraph. End of discussion." On the recording, you can hear some members of the crowd laugh in delight and excitedly clap.[14] Unfortunately, this view is all too common in the American church (and churches abroad). Many Christians, however, who value dialogue and equal opportunities based on call and gifting, don't find MacArthur's sentiments to be a laughing matter.

While up to now, this section has dealt mostly with church politics, the issue of American politics is a whole other reason why folks have left the institutional church. The short but devastating season of Trumpism and Qanon, and the reality of idolatrous Christian nationalism mixed in with an obvious Gollum-like grip on the delicacies of worldly power and white supremacy, pushed some Christians over the edge. There are some God-lovers who can't go back to a place where they perceive the revolutionary and liberating Christ is nowhere to be found.

Clone War Syndrome

There are other Christians who left the institutional church because they couldn't overcome the obstacle I call *Clone War Syndrome.* Some churches think they are in a perpetual war with the surrounding culture and with other expressions of the church. Diversity is feared and stifled for the comfort of homogeneity. These types of churches are in the business of creating clones. There is no room for messy dialogue, discussion, and dialogical encounters with people of differing theologies or ways of being in the world. It would be too anxiety-provoking and messy, especially for churches that crave safety and neat theological and moral boxes. Churches suffering from Clone War Syndrome are religious machines that seeks to bake cookie-cutter Christians.

---

14. https://www.youtube.com/watch?v=NeNKHqpBcgc

Regrettably, the cost of fear-based cloning is the stifling of creativity and curious souls. Writing about the dechurched who left the church, Packard and Hope observed, "They felt the ability to ask questions and explore various aspects of their faith wasn't supported in the church, and it was a major factor in their decisions to leave."[15] With the power of the internet, people now have the ability to travel to exotic, cognitive-dissonance-producing, theological places with the click of a button. Stale, simple, myopic, and repetitive Christian teachings on Sunday mornings are no longer going to reach the hearts and minds of many church goers. So, discouraging complex and innovative theological thought is like pouring coarse sand in the fuel tanks of the souls of thoughtful and creative people. It's true, however, that some people like things simple. But inquisitive others seek to traverse the wonders of the mind and soul, as well as all creation, for glimmers of the Divine.

In the *Bielefeld-Based Cross-Cultural Study*, another large study, researchers examined folks who deconverted from Christianity and came to similar conclusions about the unique personality and spiritual traits that prevent people from becoming passive sheep who accept church as usual. The researchers engaged in one-hundred interviews with those who left the faith either in Germany or the United States. They summarized the results:

> *The ideal deconvert would be characterized by the predominance of gains: a person who open-mindedly explores new religious orientations is ready for inter-religious encounter, rejects fundamentalism, authoritarianism and absoluteness claims, has advanced and transformed in faith development, and, especially when living in the United States, owns a strong sense of personal growth and autonomy.*[16]

15. Packard and Hope, 91.

16. Heinz Streib, Ralph W. Hood, Barbara Keller, Rosina-Martha Csoff, and Christopher F. Silver, *Deconversion: Qualitative and Quantitative Results from Cross-Cultural Research in Germany and the United States of America: Cross-Cultural Research in Germany and the United States of America* (Germany: Vandenhoeck & Ruprecht, 2009), 232.

As you can see, any type of cloning, constriction, authoritarianism, and close-mindedness is anathema to some Christ-loving folks. It is not about being overtaken by sin. It is about a spiritual ache and an evolution of consciousness. It is about people who will not settle for God-in-a-box and who desires to embrace the wondrous God of the cosmos and beyond. Here, from the Barna study, are some additional criticisms Christians gave as they unknowingly diagnosed their church with Clone War Syndrome:

- Christians demonize everything outside of the church.
- Christians are afraid of pop culture, especially its movies and music.
- Christians maintain a false separation of sacred and secular.
- Christians do not want to deal with the complexity or reality of the world.[17]

Some pastors and leaders may chalk it up to "rebellion" and "hard-heartedness to the timeless truths of God's word," but they are clearly missing the opportunity to patiently and lovingly engage with these expansive, creative, and spiritual souls. These are the same souls Packard and Hope refer to as previously being "the most dedicated people in any congregation."[18] Some church leaders don't realize that, by their refusal to change, adapt, and recontextualize the gospel message and other sacred doctrines, they are forcing people out of their congregations and creating spiritual refugees. They are inadvertently creating a new mission field. My hope is that church leaders will patiently take time to earnestly learn about the dechurched by being in close relationship with them. And I encourage church leaders to learn their language and operating system and humbly pray about how best to love them and incorporate them into the life of the church.

17. Kinnaman and Matlock, 97.

18. Packard and Hope, 23.

Moral Prescriptions

Some of the dechurched faced obstacles of moral prescriptions. These Christians were aching to be Spirit-led answer to the ills and injustices they saw in the world. They desired to be empowered, encouraged, and equipped to do good works in the community. Instead, all they heard on Sunday mornings was how to engage in a four-step sin-management plan to avoid the frightening fires of Hell. Or, if it wasn't sin-management, they were repeatedly told that the earth was going to burn down in the end times "so why be a tree hugger when people's souls were at stake?" For dechurched people, sermons were geared more toward personal holiness and eternal-torment-prevention rather than inspiring the congregation to fiercely, potently, and tangibly love others in their communities.

Packard and Hope, writing about the angst of the dechurched caused by this moral prescription dynamic, explained, "Preaching a message about the evils of drinking seemed like so much small change compared to big-ticket items such as poverty, racism, and gender inequality."[19] In other words, people's God-sized passion for issues of social justice (or simply, *God's justice*) was so great that they felt forced to leave because of the myopic, exclusivist, and narrow vision of the church. Harper, a 43-year-old Christian female, shared, "Instead of existing for the world, they exist for themselves. And that to me didn't match the biblical narrative; it didn't match what I could see was needed and possible out in the world."[20]

Diane, a retired pastor whose ministry focused on issues of social justice, wrote:

> *Why am I "done?" As an older woman, I don't find "community" in the church, especially because my friends have moved on to other, more relevant communities, or have themselves become "dones." I don't have my faith nurtured by the words, don't like being preached at, and frankly, just don't believe in the institution any more as a force for good in the world. Even before I went to seminary, I questioned much*

19. Ibid., 100.

20. Packard and Ferguson, 505.

*of the church but felt I could do more good by working within the sys-
tem than by throwing rotten tomatoes at it. And I did work within
the system for decades to try to help bring about social justice on an
institutional level. But I was just one person and eventually got tired
of butting my head up against the wall. I found I did much more good
and lived out my faith working with and for the disenfranchised of
my local society outside the walls of the church.*[21]

Shallow-itis

Another obstacle is what I call shallow-itis. For many dechurched
people, church became a place where you faked it to make it and
not a place to be real and to authentically feel. The canned sermons,
repetitive prayers, and the let's-sing-the-same-upbeat-chorus-
fifty-times worship songs, encouraged people to ignore their angst,
pain, hurt, lament, questioning, and doubts. The problem is when
church is all about positivity, singing solely upbeat music, and hearing shallow responses to complex individual and societal problems,
some Christians just can't stomach it.

Rahim, a Christian who chose to leave the institutional church
due to his encounters with "fake Christians," said, "I would rather
hang out with unbelievers than Christians because they keep it real.
I don't have to hide or pretend in front of them. And they don't
have to do that with me." Peter, a Christian who has been having a
harder and harder time remaining in church, said to me, "I feel like
church is a show. Why in the world are there fog machines and col-
ored lights with everything meticulously crafted and orchestrated
like a Broadway show? The pastor is always smiling. Christians are
always smiling. Doesn't anyone have any problems? Am I the only
one who feels like an outcast with mental health issues?"

People are looking for a holistic, real, and raw religious commu-
nity-experience. They want to worship with every last bit of their
wounded heart, fractured mind, divided soul, and lack of strength.
In their church, they never felt they had permission to do so because

21. Ibid., 509.

of the implicit rules that encouraged people to talk only about the good and to avoid the not-so-good. There are already enough shallow and oxymoronic fake-reality television shows on prime time. They are not looking for the same kind of experience in the church. With *shallow-itis* also come shallow responses to complex issues. Let's take the topic of disability in the church. Many churches are shallow in their practical aesthetic responses toward those with disabilities. And many Christians do not possess the confidence to adequately pray for those who have disabilities. When they do pray, they can recite hurtful Christian clichés that cause some to feel bad. Sometimes, Christians' verbal responses to a person's disability can be downright shallow and cruel. The late theologian Nancy L. Eiseland, born with a congenital bone defect and a strong advocate of those with disability concerns, wrote:

> As a person with a life-long disability, growing up in the church exposed me to a wide range of religious responses to disability. These folk theodicies are summed up in the familiar remarks: "You are special in God's eyes. That's why you were given this disability"; "Don't worry about your pain and suffering now, in heaven you will be made whole"; and "Thank God, it isn't worse." I was told that God gave me a disability to develop my character. But at age six or seven, I was convinced that I had enough character to last a lifetime. My family frequented faith healers with me in tow. I was never healed. People asked about my hidden sins, but they must have been so well hidden that they were misplaced even by me. The religious interpretations of disability that I heard were inadequate to my experience.[22]

Obviously, there are many reasons for Christians to be disturbed or to distance themselves from the faith they once knew. One of the most compelling reasons, shared by participants in various studies and by other well-known Christians, was the judgment they experienced from people in the church.

---

22. Nancy L. Eiesland, "Barriers and Bridges: Relating the Disability Rights Movement and Religious Organizations." In *Human Disability and the Service of God: Reassessing Religious Practice*, ed. Nancy Eiesland and Don E. Saliers (Nashville, TN: Abingdon Press, 1998), 218.

Church Should Not Feel Like a War Zone

Judgment is antithetical to building an authentic and diverse community because it is harmful to the human spirit and sabotages relational connection. Let's use technology as an example. Every time we turn on a screen, we are judged by creative, innovative advertisers who spend millions of dollars to succinctly and persuasively tell us who we are not and what we are missing. We then judge ourselves for not being attractive enough, successful enough, white enough, black enough, smart enough, hip enough, rich enough, and simply not being enough.

In the same way that we feel inadequate when we see advertisements, we may feel judgment from God for never measuring up to some unattainable religious standard. When we go to church, we expect to be challenged. Community is hard. Following Jesus can be hard. But we don't expect to be harshly judged by fellow journeyers. It seems that Christians ignore Jesus' wise encouragement to "judge not" unless we have engaged in prayerful introspection of one's own log-sized inadequacies (Matt. 7:1) or Paul's provocative, pastoral, and self-reflective question, "Who are you to judge someone else's servant?" (Rom. 14:4). Unfortunately, this is to the detriment of individual and communal flourishing.

Let me share the experiences of a few people who were judged by fellow-Christians as they traveled though their D/R season of life.

Rachel Held Evans, in her book *Searching for Sunday: Loving, Leaving, and Finding the Church*, experienced seismic shifts in her Christian faith over the years. She wrote about the judgmental responses she received from her Christian community at large:

> *My friends and professors diagnosed the crisis of faith as a deliberate act of rebellion. After graduation, rumors of my purported apostasy circulated around town, and I found myself on the prayer request lists of churches I didn't even attend. My best friend wrote me a letter*

comparing my doubts to a drug habit and explained that she needed to distance herself from me for a while.[23]

Famous Christian artist Lisa Gungor, author of *The Most Beautiful Thing I've Seen: Opening Your Eyes to Wonder,* wrote about her internalized fears of judgment because of her intense questioning of things she once held dear. Internalized fears of judgment usually have their origin from outside sources, are taken in, and are accepted as if they are a person's own ideas. Lisa wrote, "Me, the good girl once on the 'straight and narrow,' with Grammy-nominated songs and singing about God all over the world, now blinded by evil, or her evil husband, and forever to burn in the eternal pit of despair because I was doubting."[24]

Philip Salim Francis is a researcher who studied seventy-eight men and women, either graduates of Bob Jones University and Oregon Extension alumni, who grew up and embraced American evangelicalism. Francis wrote about his work in the book, *When Art Disrupts Religion: Aesthetic Experience and the Evangelical Mind.* He discovered that the arts played an instrumental role in each of the participants leaving their faith. Whether it was film, music, theatre, poetry, writing, or other creative aesthetics, the "transcendence," "real presence," "power and depth," and "wonder, awe, mystery" experienced with the arts caused them to deconstruct their conservative Christian faith.[25] The aesthetic-ruptures became born-again moments that forever changed the trajectory of their lives. In regard to the rejection the participants received because of their doubt, Philip writes, "These Bob Jones and Oregon Extension alumni almost universally claim that in the communities in which they were raised, doubting in matters of faith was frowned upon

23. Evans, 51–52.

24. Lisa Gungor, *The Most Beautiful Thing I've Seen: Opening Your Eyes to Wonder* (Grand Rapids, Michigan: Zondervan, 2018), 104.

25. Philip Salim Francis, *When Art Disrupts Religion: Aesthetic Experience and the Evangelical Mind* (New York: Oxford University Press, 2017), 3.

and doubters were regularly regarded with scorn ... Doubt was an indication of immorality."[26]

Glenn, a wild, creative pastor and a successful podcaster, who loves Jesus and the church, told of his experiences of judgment from Christians:

> *I've been unfriended and blocked by people on Facebook. I have been called a heretic, a wolf, a lost soul, a snowflake, and SJW (social justice warrior) Christian. I've been told that my thoughts are like tepid water that can't be stomached; an ear-tickler who tells people what they want to hear. A wannabe pastor. I've been ghosted by friends and other friends comment on my stuff only when they adamantly disagree with something I say.*

Marty Sampson is a well-known worship leader and avid songwriter. If you were in an evangelical church for a bit, chances are you sang a few of his songs as he wrote for Hillsong and other well-known worship bands. In August of 2019, he shocked the Christian community by stating, "I'm genuinely losing my faith"[27] and went on to describe some of his questions and doubts. His announcement was published a few days after Joshua Harris, the author of the famous and controversial book, *I Kissed Dating Goodbye*, told the world he was no longer a Christian. There was much love, grace, and overwhelming positive support for Marty, but the brutal judgment, so indicative of what many of us receive for just doubting and questioning, was downright awful. I jotted down just a few Facebook posts:

- He brought it on himself for not being rooted and grounded in love and God's word.
- He should have taken that to his pastor and started a praying session to get himself back in order.

26. Ibid., 42.

27. Michael Foust. "Hillsong's Marty Sampson: 'I'm Genuinely Losing My Faith'." ChristianHeadlines.com. Salem Web Network, August 13, 2019. https://www.christianheadlines.com/contributors/michael-foust/hillsong-s-marty-sampson-i-m-genuinely-losing-my-faith.html.

- APOSTASY is an end times sign . . . That's what's happening to Christianity. It's just that simple.
- He was never saved to begin with. Just another hell-bound hipster.
- He is just an artist and a singer . . . but never a true worshipper!
- Whatever demon has taken over his mind won't let him listen obviously.
- Go away, sort your head/heart out, come off your self-made pedestal and maybe you'll find God again. Don't lead other snowflakes into the abyss.
- Wonder why Marty Sampson is so upset. He shows he wants to be used by the devil.

Christians can be judged because of their doubts and questions, their looks, their music, their friends, their drinks, the shows and movies they watch, their social class, the politicians they choose, the amount of social justice activities they engage in, their age, their race, the amount of Bible knowledge they have, their sexual orientation, the time they spend in prayer, and the list goes on and on. As the experiences of Marty Sampson and others demonstrate, one of the most common judgments Christians face is due to their emerging beliefs.

Sociologists Packard and Hope discuss the implicit or explicit rules churches have for requiring people to align with particular beliefs before they're allowed to engage fully in the life of the church. They write, "This is not only a dubious way to practice Christianity according to our respondents, but also a profoundly ineffective way to build community."[28] A sense of community will suffer when churches focus more on propositions and theological points than on people. People are much more than brains. They are wholistic beings with varied thoughts, an assortment of backgrounds and experiences, and varied needs to uniquely express themselves. They desire to feel a sense of belonging amidst diversity

28. Packard and Hope, 40.

rather than feeling like they can only find acceptance if they believe exactly the same as everyone else.

Christians' passive-aggressive judgments are the most common and are just as painful as those that are explicitly stated. Packard and Hope write, "By far the most pervasive type of judgment our respondents described was felt or perceived rather than overtly expressed. This typically occurred between congregants and included dirty looks, ostracism, jealousy, whispering, and rumors."[29] While a lot of positive and validating encouragement come from some Christians, it is the negativity that stays with us and lingers. That is because we have what neuroscientists call a negativity bias. Rick Hanson, renowned psychologist and author of *Hardwiring Happiness,* writes, "The brain evolved a negativity bias that makes it like Velcro for bad experiences and Teflon for good ones."[30]

Our nervous system continues to remind us about the painful Velcro-prone experiences of judgment, rejection, and lack of safety. It does that to help us avoid experiencing the same distressing events over and over again. The truth is that we cannot feel a sense of belonging and safety when church life is like an emotional warzone where the bullets of critical judgment (toward the self and others) lurk around every corner. We know from a neuroscience perspective that if we do not feel safe, the part of our brain that takes in information goes offline. In other words, we can't learn if we don't feel safe around one another. It is no wonder that some of us may want to run. Christians can do better. They will need to if they want to avoid incurring more traumatized victims.

People want to experience church as a safe place to connect with God. They want an environment that can help them grow relationally and spiritually so they can make an indelible impact in the world. Judgment and rejection by those considered to be the family of God can make church and church folk feel unsafe. It could also

---

29. Ibid., 44.

30. Rick Hanson, *Hardwiring Happiness: The New Brain Science of Contentment, Calm, And Confidence* (New York: Harmony Books, 2016), xxvi.

become an obstacle to the inner transformation that is necessary for our external, Spirit-led revolutions.

YOUR D/R JOURNEY IS NOT YOUR FAULT

You may be familiar with the story in the Gospels of the Gerasene demoniac or the healing of the demon-possessed man. Parallels can be drawn between this ancient story and what has happened with contemporary spiritual refugees. Let's explore Mark's version in chapter five since, in all likelihood, Matthew and Luke copied and expanded his account.

Jesus traveled by boat with his anxious disciples across dangerous and chaotic waters to the region of the Gerasenes. Immediately, a man with an evil spirit, who was profoundly suffering and obviously not in his right mind, approached Jesus. He then fell on his knees in front of Jesus. While most people would turn away in fear or move into attack mode, Jesus didn't dismiss him, judge him, or criticize him. With profound courage and compassion, Jesus sought to address and alleviate the reasons for his suffering. Within moments, Jesus got to the bottom of his misery and the demon-possessed man was eventually healed. The man, who was once considered a monster, was miraculously "dressed and in his right mind" (v. 15) and restored to his community.

There are many perspectives one can take when reading about this man's healing. I can't help but read this story as an allegory for those who are currently suffering in the midst of their D/R journey.

I see the demon-possessed man as a person who was severely traumatized. He suffered trauma in part due to the tyranny of Roman occupation. Jesus asked him, "What is your name?" Then the demon replied, "My name is Legion, for we are many." Then Jesus sent the demons into a bunch of dirty pigs that "rushed down the steep bank into the lake and were drowned." Any hearer of this account in Jesus' time would have immediately thought of the oppressive Roman occupation. "Legion" literally meant a large number of Roman soldiers, usually around four to six thousand of them. New Testament scholar Stephen D. Moore writes about the colonial implications of Mark's narrative, "Not to put too delicate a point on it, the Romans are here shown up for the filthy swine that they are, and triumphantly driven back into the sea from whence they came—the dream of every Jewish peasant resister, as one of our own sages has observed."[31] So, as you can see, this story is not just about Jesus healing a demon-possessed man. It is a story exposing oppressive forces and subversively demonstrating the power of Jesus to heal systemic, individual, and communal trauma.

It is easy to look at individuals and blame them for their own problems and suffering. However, this story from Mark's Gospel reminds listeners after the death of Jesus, and eventually readers like us, that there are systemic and structural issues at play that wreak havoc in people's lives. The demoniac—which is a sad term because it dehumanizes the suffering person, leaves him nameless, and reduces him to a label—was living in isolation. He was staying in the "tombs" (v. 2). He "had often been chained hand and foot" (v. 4). He was in such relentless emotional pain that "he would cry out and cut himself with stones" (v. 5). Why? Was he suffering because of his genetics or the terrible sinful choices he made? Neither!

He symbolically represented all of the God-lovers in Jesus' day who were suffering due to the brutal and oppressive Roman occupation. He represented the inner anguish that occurred due to not being able to peacefully worship and live congruently in the world they inhabited. It's possible the man was suffering with what psychologists might call Dissociative Identity Disorder (DID), previously known as Multiple Personality Disorder. People experience DID when the weight of trauma becomes so severe that they are no longer able to bear it. Their psyche then fragments and splits. Actually, this is a clever defense mechanism to save the person from complete emotional annihilation. If one part/identity/personality can split and take the weight of the trauma, then the other personalities do not necessarily have to. Perhaps the violent proclivities

---

31. Stephen D. Moore, "Mark and Empire: 'Zealot' and 'Postcolonial' Readings," 134–48 in *Postcolonial Theologies: Divinity and Empire*, edited by Catherine Keller, Michael Nausner, and Mayra Rivera (St. Louis: Chalice Press, 2004), 138.

of Roman practices and barbarous persecution, where loved ones were unfairly imprisoned and lost their lives, took its toll on the demoniac.

It is also possible that the man was traumatized by members of his own community. The text tells us, "No one could bind him anymore, not even with a chain" (v. 3). Who initially put him in the dingy and desolate tomb? Who bound him with rusty and heavy chains? Was it initially done against the man's will? Could members of his own community have violently and coercively put him in the tombs just like people do to some who are mentally ill today— forcibly putting them in restraints and throwing them in a dark cell to rot in solitary confinement? Who wanted him out of sight and mind so that no one needed to bother with him?

Some people today become exceptionally worse after being in solitary confinement. Is that what happened to the man in the tombs? Could members of his own community have bruised and battered him? Could kids have come along and thrown rocks at him? After seeing Jesus come too close, was it one of his traumatized and terrorized identities who said, "Swear to God you won't torture me" (v. 8). Is this why the text says, "When they came to Jesus, they saw the man who had been possessed by the legion of demons, sitting there, dressed and in his right mind; and they were afraid." Afraid? Afraid of what? Certainly they were fearful of Jesus. After all, he just sent their precious money-making pigs (that were not exactly kosher) into the murky water to drown. But were they also afraid of what the once-possessed man might say? Were they concerned about the guilt they might have to face because of how they unlovingly treated the precious man; a man created in the image of God?

Some churches are functioning like powerful, foreign occupiers attempting to squash identities, individual desires, and anything that doesn't fit in with their pathological ideologies that masquerade as divine intentions and holy prescriptions. Consequently, an untold number of Christians are hurting today because of the sneaky leaven of burdensome and pernicious religious practices, policies, attitudes, and propositions. They are unknowingly treated like the demoniac and occupied peasants. They suffer while Christians use broad-brush and demeaning labels to "other" them. They receive various messages telling them it's their fault for distancing themselves from God (at least perceived distancing from the viewpoint of the critics) and the church:

- If you just prayed more.
- If you just fasted more.
- If you just read the Bible more.
- If you would stop sinning.
- If you would go to church more.
- If you gave more money.
- If you stopped listening to those podcasts.
- If you stopped reading those books.
- If you got rid of that unforgiveness.
- If you stopped questioning and just trusted more.

The list goes on and on. It is blame, blame, and more blame. Then, after these Christian demoniacs are traumatized and gaslit, they are passive-aggressively pushed or pressured out of the church into the darkened tombs of the world. For many, the feeling of aloneness is utterly unbearable. Some church folks hope that by distancing themselves from us heretics, they do not have to be reminded of their own lack of empathy, judgment, intolerance for diversity, cognitive dissonance, bigotry, infatuation with savior-like political leaders, hypocrisy, oppressive policies, power trips, aversion to new ideas, and overall un-Christlike ways. Sometimes, those who are traumatized simply say, "Enough!" and walk or run away.

Ironically, who may have actually been have kicked out of the church so church leaders (the occupiers) could dish out their overbearing rules, regulations, and restrictions? Could it have been . . . God? The result, both of religious foreign occupation and of kicking out Divine love, is spiritual trauma.

SPIRITUAL TRAUMA

Elizabeth Baker, a Christian writer and editor from Texas, shared how she has been negatively affected by Christian teachings and practices that do not seem to line up with the life and teachings of Jesus:

I don't sleep through the night anymore. I suffer from near daily panic attacks and almost constant anxiety. The source of my joy, my security, and my identity has vanished, leaving me with an angry grief that almost no one in my immediate circle understands. I have relationships that were once life-giving but have turned toxic. I feel manipulated, deceived, and abused. And why? The church that raised me is gaslighting me.[32]

Like Elizabeth, when people finally awaken and realize how their once-beloved faith has sadly failed them (or worse, mentally or emotionally abused them), the result can be spiritual trauma. Paul Matthew Harrison, author of *Deconversions,* writes, "When our worldview shifts or we become disillusioned with what once brought us stability, peace, comfort, and hope, it can be terribly traumatic."[33] Reba Riley, who has written about her deconstruction journey, calls the experience "Post-Traumatic Church Syndrome".[34]

Dr. Marlene Winell, psychologist and author of *Leaving the Fold: A Guide to Former Fundamentalists and Others Leaving Their Religion,* specializes in working with those who suffer due to their former religious experiences.[35] Winell calls the aftereffects of toxic religion *Religious Trauma Syndrome.* In discussing the seriousness of this tragic phenomenon—both the traumatic realization of how sick their religion made them and the process of exiting—Winell

32. Elizabeth Baker, "My Evangelical Church Is Gaslighting Me, But I Refuse to Fall For It Anymore," Huffington Post, November 28, 2018, https://www.huffpost.com/entry/evangelical-christians-trump_n_5bfc326de4b03b230fa57ae9.

33. Paul Matthew Harrison, *Deconversions: My Journey Through Evangelical Christianity* (Galena, IL: Clever Words, 2019), i.

34. See Reba Riley, *Post-Traumatic Church Syndrome: One Woman's Desperate, Funny, and Healing Journey to Explore 30 Religions by Her 30th Birthday* (New York: Howard Books, 2016).

35. Marlene Winell, *Leaving the Fold: A Guide to Former Fundamentalists and Others Leaving Their Religion* (Berkeley, CA: Apocryphile Press, 2007).

writes, "Leaving a religion, after total immersion, can cause a complete upheaval of a person's construction of reality, including the self, other people, life, and the future. People unfamiliar with this situation, including therapists, have trouble appreciating the sheer terror it can create."[36] Linda Kay Klein, author of *Pure: Inside the Evangelical Movement That Shamed a Generation of Young Women and How I Broke Free*, writes:

> *Evangelical Christianity's sexual purity movement is traumatizing many girls and maturing women haunted by sexual and gender-based anxiety, fear, and physical experiences that sometimes mimic the symptoms of post-traumatic stress disorder (PTSD). Based on our nightmares, panic attacks, and paranoia, one might think that my childhood friends and I had been to war.[37]*

YOU ARE NOT ALONE

Beloved friend, you are not crazy. There are really good reasons for why you may be experiencing the level of spiritual struggle that you are. You are a spiritual refugee. You have been forced out (or are being forced out slowly) by the church because you are different, because you are open, creative, inclusive, sensitive, and passionate, and because you have a more expansive vision for church than what a narrow-minded, judgmental, fear-based, boring, inauthentic church can provide. You have been given a scarlet letter "H" for Heretic. You have been verbally assaulted, placed in chains like you're some, wicked demoniac, and kicked to the curb like an orphaned child.

36. Valerie Tarico, "Religious Trauma Syndrome: Psychologist reveals how organized religion can lead to mental health problems," September 5, 2019, https://www.rawstory.com/2019/09/religious-trauma-syndrome-psychologist-reveals-how-organized-religion-can-lead-to-mental-health-problems/.

37. Linda Kay Klein, Pure: *Inside the Evangelical Movement That Shamed a Generation of Young Women and How I Broke Free* (New York, NY, Touchstone, An Imprint of Simon & Schuster, Inc, 2018), 8.

You are not alone. We are a part of a growing community of folks who have been hurt, disillusioned, and traumatized by some of our experiences within the Christian religion. We can't go back to the status quo. We can only deconstruct and reconstruct something more authentic and dare I say something more Christ-like.

Excerpt from the book, *Religious Refugees: (De)Constructing Toward Spiritual and Emotional Healing*, by Mark Karris, Quoir Publishing, 2020

2

THE JESUS WAY: A CREATIVE APPROACH TO READING THE SCRIPTURES

MATTHEW J. DISTEFANO

The deconstruction of one's faith is often a difficult thing to endure, not only for the person deconstructing but also for those whom they love. Any who have experienced this phenomenon, no matter which side of the table they are on, know exactly what I am talking about. Relationships can be shattered. A sense of betrayal and resentment can occur. And great loss will inevitably be suffered, typically by all parties involved.

For deconstructing Christians, a part of that great loss is the loss of the rock they once built their foundation upon. Jesus. What do they do with him when other doctrinal foundations crumble? Jesus is the main character of the Bible they, for any number of valid reasons, now don't trust, so what do they do about that? Are conservative Christians correct when they say that because he quoted from the Old Testament, he affirms everything said in it? Because of this, is Jesus not to be trusted as well? Should the baby indeed be thrown out with the tepid bathwater?

My goal in this essay is to provide some relief from nagging questions such as these. It will be my hope that for those struggling with the Scriptures, these pages can lend some aid. By the end of reading it, perhaps you'll even conclude something similar to what I have concluded, which is that we don't have to trust the Bible. We just need to put it in its proper place and know how to read like more creatively, like Jesus did. To that end, for the remainder of this essay, we will explore four instances where Jesus took creative liberty with the Scriptures, and then follow that up by exploring how Paul took the same approach. (Note: It may help to have a Bible handy for the remainder of this essay.)

JESUS

Instance 1: Luke 4:16–30, Referencing Isaiah 61:1–2

Allow me to set the scene. We begin in Luke 3, where Jesus is baptized by John the Baptist. Filled with the Holy Spirit, Jesus then heads out into the wilderness (Luke 4:1). Here, he is tested by the devil. But, like a Kung Fu master, Jesus dismisses Satan, passing the ultimate spiritual test. While in the power of the Spirit, Jesus then heads to the synagogue in Nazareth to proclaim the jubilant good news that he is about to bring. When he arrives, he opens the scroll of the prophet Isaiah, turning right to the Jubilee text from chapter 61 (one of everyone's favorites), and reads:

The Spirit of the Lord is upon me,
Because he has anointed me
To bring good news to the poor.
He has sent me to proclaim release to the captives
And recovery of sight to the blind,
To Let the oppressed go free,
To proclaim the year of the Lord's favor.

– LUKE 4:18–19

Rolling up the scroll, Jesus makes a full stop, midsentence, and boldly proclaims, "Today this scripture has been fulfilled in your hearing" (Luke 4:21). Then, in the very next verse, *you-know-what* hits the fan. And before you retort by saying "that's not what the next verse says," let me clarify something.

In Luke 4:22, the passage in most biblical translations indeed reads "all spoke well of him," but in all reality, the Greek text simply says πάντες ἐμαρτύρουν αὐτῷ, or "all bore witness to him."[38] So what is going on here? Scholar Michael Hardin, in his masterful work *The Jesus Driven Life*, offers a compelling answer:

> *Translators have to make what is known as a syntactical decision, they have to decide whether or not the "bearing witness" is negative or positive. Technically speaking they have to decide if the dative pronoun "to him" is a dative of disadvantage or a dative of advantage; was the crowd bearing witness to his advantage or to his disadvantage?*[39]

In other words, translators have to make a choice: Was the crowd enthralled with Jesus' message, bearing positive witness, and proud that Jesus was Joseph's son? Or, rather, were they upset by it, and bore negative witness to it by dismissing Jesus as the son of a "nobody?" (After all, as John 1:46 teaches, nothing good ever came out of Nazareth.) Well, it seems that based on Jesus' sarcastic

---

38. The KJV actually gets this correct, and reads "And all bare him witness." However, most translations, such as the NRSV and NIV, add their own personal interpretation and render it "all spoke well of him."

39. Hardin, *Jesus Driven Life*, 67.

response in vv. 23–27 that the latter is more accurate. Otherwise, why would he get defensive for seemingly no reason? It is doubtful he would. Instead, it seems more reasonable to think that Jesus is responding to the jeering crowd in front of him. The reverse makes little contextual sense.

But a key question remains: *Why* were they so pissed off to begin with? What gets them all riled up in the first place? The answer, to put it plainly, is in how Jesus reads from the text from Isaiah. Notice, in Isaiah 61:2, a key feature to the Jubilee passage is "the day of vengeance of our God." But Jesus does not read this part. In fact, he stops midsentence in order to omit the theological claim that God was going to bring vengeance down upon the very people he, as well as the prophets Elijah and Elisha before him, were sent by God to bless. For Jesus, unlike his interlocutors, God was *not* going to deliver his people from Roman occupation through the use of vengeance; instead, he was going to bring good news to *all* the poor, proclaim release to *all* the captives, recovery of sight to *all* the blind; he was going to let *all* the oppressed go free, and proclaim the year of the Lord's favor without any such eschatological violence.

This is what gets the crowd in a tizzy. And that is why they then "bear witness" to Jesus, not advantageously, but disadvantageously. They are upset over Jesus' omission of a very key part of the Isaianic text, which leads them to sarcastically dismiss Jesus as merely "the son of Joseph," or in other words, the son of a "nobody" (cf. John 1:46). Hence Jesus' retort: "No prophet is accepted in the prophet's hometown" (Luke 4:24).

To sum this all up: What the people cannot accept here is a teacher who teaches that a Day of Jubilee is a day *without* "the vengeance of our God" (Isa. 61:2). It is such an offensive claim, in fact, that they nearly throw Jesus off a cliff because of it (Luke 4:29–30). Indeed, Jesus must have learned, that very day, just how dangerous it is to mess with folks' presupposed doctrines.

Instance 2: Luke 7:18–23, Referencing Various Passages from Isaiah; 1 and 2 Kings

Here's our second scene. John the Baptist is in a bit of a pickle. He really wants to know if Jesus is the messiah, "the one who is to come" (Luke 7:20). But he is also in prison for speaking out against King Herod and his minions. So, to solve this conundrum, John sends some of his disciples to speak with Jesus in order to clarify just who Jesus really is. However, when John's disciples reach Jesus and ask John's questions, Jesus, in typical Jesus-fashion, does not simply answer *yes* or *no*, but instead offers a multilayered and highly technical response.

The answer Jesus provides primarily consists of scriptural quotations from Isaiah (and some from First and Second Kings). He informs the disciples to tell John that the blind receive sight (Isa 29:18; 35:5; 61:1–2), the lame walk (Isa 35:6), the lepers are cleansed (2 Kgs 5:1–27), the deaf hear (Isa 29:18; 35:5), the dead are raised (1 Kgs 17:17–34), and the poor have good news brought to them (Isa 29:19). Like the story from Luke 4, though, there is something going on under the surface that we must pay attention to.

You see, John the Baptist most likely shared a similar eschatology with the folks in Nazareth—the ones who were ready to throw Jesus from a cliff for his elimination of "the day of vengeance of our God" from Second Isaiah. We see evidence of this in Luke 3:7–9, where John warns the people of "the wrath to come."[40] So, it's quite telling that when Jesus quotes the above Isaianic passages, he always eliminates the associated vengeance texts.

See for yourself. Isaiah 29:18–19 is referenced, but not Isaiah 29:20: ~~"For the tyrant shall be no more, and the scoffer shall cease to be; all those alert to do evil shall be cut off"~~; Isaiah 35:5–6 is included, but not Isaiah 35:4: ~~"Here is your God. He will come with vengeance, with terrible recompense"~~; and Isaiah 61:1–2 is used, but not the phrase "and the day of vengeance of our God" from v. 2.[41]

---

40. Ibid., 70.

41. Ibid., 69–70.

Then, Jesus does a mic drop, when he concludes with: "And blessed is anyone who takes no offense at me" (Luke 7:23). The offense he is talking about here is the same offense caused in the synagogue in Nazareth. It is the offense, or scandal, of a non-vengeful Father. But, for those who are not offended, they will find blessing here, because they will see that God indeed blesses everyone. That is the exact message Jesus gives in Matthew 5:45, when he teaches that God "sends rain on the righteous and on the unrighteous"—which, by the way, is a direct subversion of the very Deuteronomic God Jesus' contemporaries so often affirmed, the God who were told will "change the rain of your land into powder, and only dust shall come down upon you from the sky until you are destroyed." (Deut. 28:24)

Instance 3: Matthew 5, Referencing Leviticus 24:20; Various Passages from Deuteronomy 28

Scene three: The Sermon on the Mount. Here, Jesus makes some very interesting statements that should garner our attention. On a number of occasions, he begins a teaching with "You have heard that it was said, but I say to you." What this means is that he is going to be quoting from his Scriptures, and then follow that with a fresh take on how to apply the instructions. So, for instance, contrary to Leviticus 24:20, in Matthew 5:38–39, Jesus says "You have heard that it was said, 'An eye for an eye and a tooth for a tooth,' but I say to you, Do not resist an evildoer. But, if anyone strikes you on the right cheek, turn the other also." However, Jesus also qualifies these teachings with the statement: "Do not think that I have come to abolish the law or the prophets; I have not come to abolish, but to fulfill" (Matt. 5:17).

So, what is going on here?

First off, we have to figure out if by "fulfill" Jesus meant that he came to affirm every jot and tittle in the whole of the "law and prophets," or that he came to perfect and complete them. This is to ask, is Jesus simply agreeing with all the teachings of Moses and the other Hebrew writers, or is he the telos, or ultimate goal, of them? To address this, we should simply ask ourselves this: how did Jesus interpret the passages he quotes?

Well, given his direct "contradiction"—or, rather, expansion—
of multiple teachings (namely those from Lev. 24:20; Deut. 28:15,
20–24, 59–61; Eccles. 5:4), we should conclude the latter; that
Jesus is not necessarily affirming the letter of every law, but the
spirit behind the whole of it. In other words, when we say that
Jesus fulfills the Law, what we're not saying is that every theological datum in the whole of the Law and prophets must be affirmed,
but that the whole of Israel's story points to one thing: Christ. And,
more specifically, peace through Christ. As René Girard points out:
"When Jesus declares that he does not abolish the Law but fulfills
it, he articulates a logical consequence of his teaching. The goal of
the Law is peace among humankind."[42]

That is the key right there!

The Law's command to take "an eye for an eye and a tooth for
a tooth," rather than being viewed as simply an archaic form of
justice, should be viewed as a mandate that actually attempts to get
to the root of the problem—violence. That is to say, it takes us from
a more violent place to a less violent one. Remember, once Abel's
blood is spilled, vengeance is taken by Lamech—who is only a few
generations removed from Abel—seventy times sevenfold (Gen.
4:23–24). That is quite a bit more excessive than "an eye for an
eye," is it not? Because of this, a flood of violence ensues, wiping
out almost all of humanity. To stop such chaos, Mosaic Law gets
to the heart of the matter by saying "stop at an eye for an eye," but
simply cannot quite do the job. Jesus, however, as the telos of the
Law, does. And he does so by teaching that we should not resist[43]

---

42. Girard, *I See Satan*, 14.

43. What Jesus is not saying is that Christians are to allow themselves and others to be
persecuted. Regarding Jesus' command to non-resistance, Michael Hardin points out,
"The Greek verb used (antistenai) does not mean be a doormat, it means that when you
are abused (persecuted), you 'speak truth to power' by engaging in actions which, while
nonviolent, are also resistant. Turning the other cheek does not mean letting someone
strike you over and over. It is a way of calling attention to the abuse in a nonviolent
fashion such that the abuser will recognize the futility of their actions." (Hardin, *Jesus
Driven Life*, 126) See, also, Walter Wink's *Engaging the Powers*, pp 175–77.

our persecutors (Matt. 5:38–42), that we should love our enemies (v.44), and pray for them, and that we should be perfect, just as our heavenly Father is perfect (v.48). In Luke's version of the sermon, the Father's mercy is the lynchpin of perfection (Luke 6:36), thus showing how mercy and love go hand in hand, and that they are to take precedence over retributive justice.

So, does Jesus abolish the Law? No, of course not. Abolishment means that something ends prematurely. He fulfills and exegetes it perfectly. And in doing so, he models a perfect theological framework by showing how God is best defined by his perfect love of enemies (Matt. 5:43–48) and mercy for the wicked (Luke 6:36). And he shows that although it may not have always been the Moses way—although it is at times—it is in fact the truly human and therefore truly divine Way.

Instance 4: Luke 20:41–47, Referencing Psalm 110:1

This scene begins with "the chief priests and the scribes" questioning Jesus (Luke 20:1). These folks had a tendency for doing such a thing. And not only that, but they also had a tendency to proof-text the Torah during their interrogations, often times in order to then clobber people over the head (John 8:3–5). This led to some atrocious sociological implications (women being stoned to death, for example).

Adding fuel to the fire, in the minds of some, Israel's future king—the messianic deliverer who would free the Jews from the grip of Roman Law—was soon coming with violence and vengeance, and from the house of David (2 Sam. 7:1–17). In spite of Jerusalem being destroyed by the Babylonians in 586 BCE, which forced the Israelites into exile for the next five-hundred or so years, many still believed in this deliverance to come. And that meant there would be hell to pay for Israel's enemies. The Pharisees, no doubt, would have been familiar with this notion, and so too Jesus. In fact, Jesus—while not affirming all the presupposed ideas about what messiahship meant—does accept this title in Mark 14:62.

So, with these two things in mind—the Pharisaical approach to the Scriptures as well as the Davidic understanding of

Messiah—let's get to the passage at-hand, because what Jesus does with the Pharisees' inquires is nothing short of brilliant.

After Jesus puts the scribes in their place, Luke tells us how "they no longer dared to ask him another question" (Luke 20:40). Jesus then poses his own rhetorical question: "How can they say that the Messiah is David's son?" Well, certainly Jesus knew that the Messiah would come from the Davidic line, so where is Jesus going with this? What is he up to, asking such a rhetorical question? He continues:

> For David himself says in the book of the Psalms,
> "The Lord said to my Lord,
> Sit at my right hand,
> Until I make your enemies your footstool."

> – LUKE 20:41–43

Let's unpack this by focusing on two distinct things.

First, in Psalm 110:1—the passage being quoted by Jesus— the traditional understanding of this passage is that the first "Lord" mentioned is to be understood as God, while the second is either David or one of his descendants (i.e., a future king).[44]

But this is read differently by Jesus.

When Jesus gets a hold of this passage, he names David as the first "Lord"—for David himself says—and the future Messiah (Jesus) as the second. Jesus then asks, "How can they say that the Messiah is David's son?" Why does he ask this? Because, for David to call one of his descendants "lord," it is only because that descendant was special in some way, that he was deserving of such a title— you simply did not call your sons and other descendants "lord." To that end, when Jesus attaches himself to the second "lord," he is making a dangerously bold move, not only because he tinkers with Scripture in order to do so, but because he is not held in too high of esteem amongst the scribes and Pharisees. If you recall, it is only a few verses prior that they had sent spies to watch Jesus in order

44. Enns, *The Bible Tells Me So*, 176.

to trap him so as to hand him over to the Roman authorities (Luke 20:20). So, for Jesus to attach himself to the concept of "messiah?" Whoa boy, watch out; things are about to get real!

Second, when Jesus quotes from Psalm 110, he again omits any of the associated vengeance texts (Ps. 110:2–3, 5–7). In fact, any time Psalm 110 is quoted in the New Testament, Psalm 110:2–3, 5–7 is always omitted (Heb. 5:6; 6:20; 7:17, 21). This is important because crucial to any Davidic understanding of messiahship is a Rambo-style deliverance—think along the lines of Mark Driscoll's Jesus: "a Pride fighter with a tattoo down his leg, a sword in his hand and the commitment to make someone bleed."[45] It certainly seems like that is what John the Baptist was expecting (Luke 3:7–9). And it is definitely what the folks in Nazareth were waiting for (Luke 4:18–30). But, by attaching himself to the concept of Messiah, and then by again omitting all of the associated vengeance passages from his quotations of Scripture, Jesus reorients the assumed understanding of "divine deliverance." Yes, the Messiah may in fact be from the Davidic line (although perhaps not in the traditional sense), but he will not be a Davidic warrior-type, and he will not be bringing vengeance upon his enemies. Instead, he will love his enemies and pray for those who persecute him (Matt 5:44). In fact, Jesus' last prayer prior to his final breath is for the forgiveness of those who declared him an enemy: "Father forgive them; for they do not know what they are doing (Luke 23:34)." What a complete reversal of what Messiah was to be viewed as, a Christology that is a complete rejection of militarism and violent deliverance!

45. From an interview with *Relevant Magazine*, which can be found at http://www.relevant-magazine.com/god/church/features/1344-from-the-mag-7-big-questions.

PAUL

Instance 5: Galatians 3:10–13, Referencing Deuteronomy 21:23

Paul's letter to the Galatians is one of my favorites. Perhaps it is because we can easily tell just how pissed off Paul is. And, if I'm being honest, that is one of the reasons I like him so much. Like me, he defends the Gospel by telling it like it is and has a bit of a snarky streak. I mean, it is not that often you hear good men of God sarcastically wishing for teachers of false gospels to castrate themselves (Gal. 5:12). The last I checked, telling church leaders to cut off their genitalia was frowned upon.

Nevertheless, allow me to offer a brief contextual note so that we can address the passage at-hand.

What is specifically going on in this letter is that Paul is upset by a group of teachers from the Jerusalem Church who are espousing a counterfeit, Jewish-Christian message to his churches in Galatia and elsewhere (Gal. 1:7; cf. Rom. 16:17). Peter, at least indirectly, is included among these.[46] What is being falsely taught is that prior to becoming a follower of Christ, one had to comply with Mosaic Law: obey the Sabbath, keep a kosher table (Gal. 2:11–12), and, if male, become circumcised (Acts 11:2–3; 15:1–2). Furthermore, it seems this false message included some harsh and unfair rhetoric levied against Gentiles.[47] This leads to division in the Church, and really pisses Paul off because for him, there were to be absolutely no dividing lines (Gal. 3:28; Rom. 10:12), and anything "of the Law" is not to be held in too high esteem—as it brings a curse (Gal. 3:10), on Christ even (Gal. 3:13), wrath (Rom. 4:15), and death (Rom. 7:9–10; 8:2). Hence the reason for Paul's rhetoric against the false teachers and their law-based "gospel" in Galatians 5:12: "I

---

46. Martyn, *Galatians*, 246–47.

47. Evidence for this can be found in Romans 1:18–32, as well as Galatians 5:19–21. In both instances, Paul is rhetorically playing the role of the false teacher and quotes traditional anti-Gentile rhetoric that can be found in Wisdom of Solomon 13–14, but in other places as well. (Campbell, *Deliverance of God*, 360–62)

wish those who unsettle you would castrate themselves!" In essence,
I believe Paul is saying: If you are going to force people to cut off
the tips of their penises in order to be "justified" before God and
the Law, then why don't you just go ahead and cut off your own
penis instead!

With this brief contextual note in mind, let's turn to a passage in
Galatians where Paul employs a creative interpretation of a familiar
phrase from the book of Deuteronomy. He does this in order to
condemn the very Law that the false teachers are using in their
condemnation of others—which, incidentally, by its very logic, condemns the false teachers themselves (cf. Rom. 2:1).

Notice how, in Galatians 3:10, Paul emphatically states that the
law—which, by the way, Pauline scholar J. Louis Martyn argues
was given at Sinai in God's absence (Gal. 3:19–20)[48]—is a curse to
everyone who relies on it (Gal. 3:10). Why? Because the Scriptures
are clear: everyone will fall short in one way or another (Rom. 3:23)
and the minute that happens is the minute you are under its curse
(Gal. 3:10; cf. Deut. 28:15, 20–24, 59–61).

After establishing this sobering truth, Paul then lays down
the gauntlet by creatively quoting Deuteronomy 21:23, writing:
"Cursed is everyone who hangs on a tree" (Gal. 3:13). What Paul
fails to include in that phrase is the kicker. Notice the difference:

Deuteronomy 21:23: "For anyone hung on a tree is under *God's
curse*" (emphasis mine)

Galatians 3:13: "Cursed is everyone who hangs on a tree."

Did you catch that? For the writer of the book of Deuteronomy—
as well as all the penal substitution folks— God's curse is upon
anyone who is hung on a tree. But, for Paul, that is not so. In fact,
he says that nobody speaking by the Spirit of God says "Jesus is
cursed," only that he is Lord (1 Cor. 12:3). Yet cursed and hung
upon a tree is exactly where Jesus ends up anyway—with help
from the Law, no less. So, what Paul understands is that it is not
God who is the architect of such cursing— as God does not create

48. Martyn, *Galatians*, 364–70.

systems that lead to the killing of his very own son—but rather, the Law is. Or, to put it really simply, humanity and its systems cursed Jesus. Yet, because he was truly innocent, God raised him from the dead (Gal. 1:1); which he would have never done had he really been cursed by God.

Instance 6: Romans 15:7–13, Referencing Various Passages from Psalm 18; Deuteronomy 32:43

We again turn to the Apostle Paul, but this time to his letter to the Romans. It is a most difficult letter to interpret and has given scholars and lay Christians alike fits for millennia. Perhaps it is one of the letters Peter is referring to in 2 Peter 3:16, when he writes, "There are some things in them [Paul's letters] hard to understand." So, for our purposes, we are going to have to make an assumption, namely that Pauline scholar Douglas Campbell is essentially correct in how to best approach it. As a non-scholar myself, I realize that, inevitably, trust will have to be placed in another who is above my pay grade. Do we all not have to do this in some regard? I am not making a blind assumption though. Rather, it is the result of years of diligent study. Perhaps I am wrong, but you will have to decide that for yourself.

So, here's the gist of how Romans is to be approached, according to Campbell and others.[49]

In *The Deliverance of God*, Campbell argues that, instead of all of Romans 1–4 being entirely the "voice of Paul," it is a "dialogue" between Paul and the false teachers we just discussed—those who were either in Rome or on their way to Rome at the time of this letter. Campbell sums up his method for approaching the first four chapters of the letter:

> *There are certain instances where Paul attributes material to the Teacher directly, using the technique of prosopopoeia. In these texts*

---

49. Those who come to mind include, but are not limited to, J. Louis Martyn and Chris Tilling.

the Teacher in effect speaks for himself (although suitably crafted by Paul, of course)—first in the opening of his usual conversion speech (1:18–32), and then later in dialogue with Paul (3:1–9). However, for much of the rest of the argument Paul is quoting the Teacher's teaching, and rather sarcastically, and this is entirely consistent with his main rhetorical goal throughout the section, which is to refute the Teacher in terms of his own gospel.[50]

Remember, this so-called "gospel" is the Jewish-centered one, which, in all reality, is entirely counterfeit (Gal. 1:6–7). In addition to keeping various Jewish laws, this false gospel comes chock full of anti-Gentile rhetoric, typical of some prominent Jewish sentiments (cf. Wisdom of Solomon 13–14). This rhetoric can be found scattered all throughout Romans 1:18–32. And crucial to this message is the commonly held Jewish belief that "the wrath of God" will be revealed against those Gentiles who practice these abominable things (Rom. 1:18).

But here's where things get good.

Paul, in order to show how false this "gospel" truly is, then turns it right back around on the false teachers in Rom 2:1: "*Therefore you have no excuse, whoever you are, when you judge others; for in passing judgment on another you condemn yourself, because you, the judge, are doing the very same things.*" (Emphasis mine) Basically, what he is arguing is that if the wrath of God is going to be revealed—just as the false gospel says it is (Rom. 1:18)—it will be revealed against the false teachers, too. There is a qualification, however, because in all reality, it will not be the "wrath of God" that befalls the teachers, but wrath stored up by themselves for their insistence on preaching and practicing the gospel of wrath (Rom. 2:5). In effect, Paul is saying that you reap what you sow, and if you are going to sow a law-based, wrathful gospel, that is what you are going to reap upon yourself.

That being said, let's move on to my main point, which is that Paul then later uses a specific hermeneutical method—similar to that of Jesus in Luke 7:22—as further evidence that the true Gospel is wholly inclusive to Gentiles, and that the false, wrathful, law-based message of the teachers is dead on arrival. What he specifically does is quote the Hebrew Scriptures, and then exegetes them so he can point to a time where Gentiles "might glorify God for his *mercy*" (Rom. 15:9, emphasis mine). First up, Romans 15:9b (quoting Psalm 18:49): "Therefore I will confess you among the Gentiles, and sing praises to your name." What is left off, of course, is all of the vengeful passages that precede this declaration: "~~They cried for help, but there was no one to save them; they cried to the Lord, but he did not answer them. I beat them fine, like dust before the wind; I cast them out like the mire of the streets~~ … ~~Blessed be~~ … ~~the God who gave me vengeance and subdued peoples under me~~" (Ps. 18:41–42, 46–47). Then, one verse later (quoting Deuteronomy 32:43): "And again he says, 'Rejoice, O Gentiles, with his people." And again, what is left off is the vengeance that follows: "~~For he will avenge the blood of his children, and take vengeance on his adversaries; he will repay those who hate him, and cleanse the land for his people.~~"

This consistent interpretive pattern is, again, for the purpose of eliminating the dividing lines that certain Jewish-Christians were creating in the first century. Being falsely taught was that one must obey the Law—kosher table, Sabbath, and penis slicing—in order to have the Gospel. And Paul was having none of it, because, for Paul, to take away the truth of the Gospel with laws fabricated in God's absence (Gal. 3:19–20[51]) was to preach a false gospel and thus pronounce judgment on all, including one's self (Rom. 2:1). Or, in other words, to store up self-inflicted wrath (Rom. 2:5).

Yet, for Paul, in spite of all this, due to the fact that all of us, both Jew and Gentile, are so damn disobedient (Rom. 11:30– 31), God will be merciful to all whom he pleases, that is, all (Rom. 11:32). This even includes the false teachers! That's just how inclusive Paul's theology is. Indeed, it's a theology centered on the mercy of God: "For

---

51. Martyn, *Galatians*, 364–70.

God has imprisoned all in disobedience so that he may be merciful to all." (Rom. 11:32) Hence the jubilant exaltation at the very end of his rhetorical argument (which runs from Romans 9–11):

> O the depth of the riches and wisdom and knowledge of God! How unsearchable are his judgments and how inscrutable his ways! "For who has known the mind of the Lord? Or who has been his counselor? Or who has given a gift to him, to receive a gift in return?" For from him and through him and to him are all things. To him be the glory forever. Amen."

– ROMANS 11:33–36

Instance 7: Ephesians 6:13–17, Referencing Isaiah 59:17–18

Ephesians 6:13–17 is a passage from Paul that should be familiar to any Christian. It reads:

> Therefore take up the whole armor of God, so that you may be able to withstand on that evil day, and having done everything, to stand firm. Stand therefore, and fasten the belt of truth around your waist, and put on the breastplate of righteousness. As shoes for your feet put on whatever will make you ready to proclaim the gospel of peace. With all of these, take the shield of faith, with which you will be able to quench all the flaming arrows of the evil one. Take the helmet of salvation, and the sword of the Spirit, which is the word of God.

What many of us may not realize is that this is a direct reference to Isaiah 59:17–18. However, like so many other instances, there is going to be some tinkering done by Paul. Sure, the "breastplate of righteousness" and "helmet of salvation" are included in Paul's version of the armor of God, but notice what is, not coincidentally, missing:

> He put on garments of vengeance for clothing,
> and wrapped himself in fury as a mantle.
> According to their deeds, so he will repay;
> wrath to his adversaries, requital to his enemies.

—ISAIAH 59:17B–18

Indeed, as Paul notes, there is armor to be put on, for there is a war at-hand. However, this is not a war of "blood and flesh," but a war fought against the "cosmic powers of this present darkness, against the spiritual forces of evil in the heavenly places (Eph. 6:12)." It is not a war to be fought with literal swords, bows and arrows, but a "sword of the Spirit, which is the word of God." And for this war we bear no garments of vengeance, no boots of war; rather, we gird our bare feet with the "gospel of peace."

CONCLUDING THOUGHTS

In this essay, my goal was to point to some of the direct evidence that both Jesus and the apostle Paul had a method for interpreting the Hebrew Bible. In essence, what we saw was how both draw out the best of their Scriptures in order to point to a heavenly Father who is non-sacrificial, non-vengeful, and non-violent.

To that end what I want to emphasize is this: To take the Bible seriously is to not take everything literally. Sure, some things we should take literally. Jesus told us to literally love our enemies (Matt. 5:44; Luke 6:35); he told us to literally bless those who curse us (Luke 6:28); he told us to literally turn the other cheek (Matt. 5:39); and he told us to literally be merciful just like our heavenly Father is (Matt. 5:48; Luke 6:36). But, as for some of the other stuff that we've said about God over the millennia—even if we've said it in the Bible—well, now that's a different story. Some of that has to be modified in light of Jesus, the most unexpected of messiahs.

Adapted from the book, *Heretic! An LGBTQ-Affirming, Divine Violence-Denying, Christian Universalist's Responses to Some of Evangelical Christianity's Most Pressing Concerns,* by Matthew J. Distefano, Quoir Publishing, 2018

3

DOUBT EVERYTHING

MATTHEW J. KORPMAN

"If doubt appears, it should not be considered as the negation of faith, but as an element which was always and will always be present in the act of faith."

– Paul Tillich

Let me start this chapter by asking a trick question: which disciple doubted Jesus' resurrection? If you're like most, you'll probably shout "Thomas!" Most would. Many preachers do. Of course, depending on where you are reading this, shouting may not be advisable. Anyway, the point is that you'd be partially wrong. The question was a trick because "disciple" should be in the plural. While it is true that Thomas doubted Jesus' resurrection (and we'll get to him in a bit), he wasn't the only one who did. In fact, a great number of

Jesus' disciples doubted Christianity's central event! In the Gospel of Matthew, at the close of his story, we read the following stunning and baffling account:

> Now the eleven disciples went to Galilee, to the mountain to which Jesus had directed them. When they saw him, they worshiped him; but some doubted. And Jesus came and said to them, "All authority in heaven and on earth has been given to me. Go therefore and make disciples of all nations, baptizing them in the name of the Father and of the Son and of the Holy Spirit, and teaching them to obey everything that I have commanded you. And remember, I am with you always, to the end of the age."
>
> – MATTHEW 28:16–20[52]

This is supposed to be the greatest moment of Christianity, in which the disciples behold Jesus rising with the angels to his heavenly throne, fully alive and having conquered death. And what does Matthew's Gospel tell us about this powerful moment of faith? *Some doubted.* Watching their master and rabbi ascend into the sky, those closest to Christ doubted. What did they doubt? Apparently, everything. I'm certain that this is shocking for some of you to imagine, especially if you have been brought up believing that such behavior is wrong to have as a person of faith.

But, *here's the rub* (as John Collins is fond of saying in his classes at Yale): regardless of the doubts of the disciples, Jesus still commissions and empowers them. Their doubts about his resurrection, even as the ascending Jesus stares down at them, do not prevent them from being Christ's apostles. Their doubts are not said to be solved or dealt with, and yet, even so, Jesus sends them out on his behalf, promising to be with them "to the end of the age." In the midst of their doubting, Jesus commissions them to be his disciples. In other words, he accepts them and commissions them to take those doubts and utilize them in service toward the one they doubt. If that was

52. As a general note, all quotations from the Bible will be drawn from the New Revised Standard Version (NRSV), unless otherwise noted. All italics within biblical quotes are added by me for emphasis.

powerful two thousand years ago to Jewish and Gentile readers, it is certainly just as powerful in today's *post*-postmodern society.

GOD WANTS YOU TO DOUBT

Which leads us to another biblical bombshell: God doesn't just overlook our doubts, he encourages them. Paul once wrote in 1 Thess. 5:21 that the early Christians should *"doubt everything, and keep what is good."* It's a verse that seems perfect for our postmodern age, yet most Christians never hear it in church. The Greek word δοκιμάζω (*dokimazo*) is often translated in Bibles as "test," but the meaning is given variously by biblical dictionaries as "to try and determine the genuineness of," to determine its "acceptance as trustworthy," to "discern" or to "verify." All of which ultimately means that in order to test everything, you must also test things that you already believed were proven. And that inevitably means that you must question certain things, things that you never had reason to doubt before, with a healthy dose of skepticism. And like a series of links in a chain, one realizes that in order to question whether your legs can lift your weight (something most take for granted), one must be willing to consider the possibility that your legs might not be able to. To test means *to question*, and to question means *to doubt* (if done sincerely, rather than jestingly).

Paul's advice is not for Christians to simply become skeptics who throw their hands up in the air (enough people today already do that), but it is a cautious warning to realize that all of our beliefs and ideas (even about the Bible) require testing (which begins with doubting) in order to throw away what is no longer needed and "keep what is good." That last statement by Paul is important as well, since he affirms that we will often find good things mixed with not-so-good things. We are not advised to throw away the good just because of the bad. And while this is certainly true of many things in life, I especially believe the same is true of Scripture, which is why Paul affirms that we "should *try* to find out what is pleasing to the LORD," but stops short of saying that it is something we can easily do even when reading our scriptures (Eph. 5:10). And in Romans 14 he goes so far as to state that if Christians cannot come to one interpretation, God isn't ultimately concerned with whether they do or don't (vss. 22–23).

It's a shocking idea for some. Does God really leave room for us to question and to doubt? Does the Bible encourage questions rather than quickly attempt to solve them? The answer is yes! Rather than being a sin, it is God's delight for us to question what he says. And moreover, I firmly believe that once we have this principle in our minds, we can begin to move forward and become (re) introduced to the Bible that we either are learning about for the first time or are falling back in love with once again.

CERTAINTY IS A PROBLEM

It's fascinating to note that in the Gospel of Luke, the disciples are said to doubt even earlier than Matthew's account had alluded. In fact, in Luke's account, not just *some*, but *all* of the disciples doubt Jesus' resurrection.

> *While they were talking about this, Jesus himself stood among them and said to them, "Peace be with you." They were startled and terrified, and thought that they were seeing a ghost. He said to them, "Why are you frightened, and why do doubts arise in your hearts? Look at my hands and my feet; see that it is I myself. Touch me and see; for a ghost does not have flesh and bones as you see that I have." And when he had said this, he showed them his hands and his feet. While in their joy they were disbelieving and still wondering, he said to them, "Have you anything here to eat?" They gave him a piece of broiled fish, and he took it and ate in their presence.*

> – LUKE 24:36–43

Gathered together, Jesus' inner circle of eleven (minus Judas), come face to face with the risen Christ. Unlike the previous account, this one gives more details about the questions on their minds. According to Luke, the object of all the disciples' doubts was whether Jesus was a ghost (and indeed dead), or whether he was resurrected (and indeed alive). They cannot bring themselves to believe that he not only *appeared* to them, but that he is physically present among them.

Again though, Jesus does not judge them, nor does he reprimand their disbelief. Instead, he asks for food to demonstrate that he is alive and physically with them. He understands his followers' questions and willingly attempts to provide what they desire and need. Their very doubts lead them into a better understanding of the risen Jesus.

It is within *this* context that we find John's account of Thomas, and it is only within this context that we can start to appreciate what John is doing in his narrative.

> But Thomas (who was called the Twin), one of the twelve, was not with them when Jesus came. So, the other disciples told him, "We have seen the LORD." But he said to them, "Unless I see the mark of the nails in his hands, and put my finger in the mark of the nails and my hand in his side, I will not believe." A week later his disciples were again in the house, and Thomas was with them. Although the doors were shut, Jesus came and stood among them and said, "Peace be with you." Then he said to Thomas, "Put your finger here and see my hands. Reach out your hand and put it in my side. Do not doubt but believe." Thomas answered him, "My LORD and my God!" Jesus said to him, "Have you believed because you have seen me? Blessed are those who have not seen and yet have come to believe."
>
> – JOHN 20:24–29

If you're like me, you've probably heard this story told from the pulpit a thousand times. "Remember Jesus' words," preachers remind their congregants, "Don't be a doubting Thomas. Believe!" The entire story is transformed into a condemnation of questioning and doubt. Yet, these sermons do a great disservice to this story, distorting its meaning. For the message of this story in John neither condemns Thomas for his doubt nor does it present Thomas as the only doubter.

The event in John's story is the same as Luke's. They are both attempting to narrate the same thing. So, it is with great interest that we can note that when these two accounts are placed together, it becomes clear that not only Thomas, but *all* the disciples doubted

Jesus. His words then are not directed to Thomas, but all the disciples as a whole. However, we don't actually need Luke's account to show this to be true. Even John's Gospel reveals the same set of facts all on its own terms.

To begin, the story in John 20 opens with the note in verse 18 that Mary had told the fearful disciples that she had seen Jesus and that he was ascending to his reign in heaven. Yet what does the text tell us next? We are informed that the disciples are still hiding in fear within the room. Does this sound like the reaction of those who believe Mary? No, certainly not. Only a few verses earlier, it mentions in John's Gospel that the disciples doubted Mary's initial report that the tomb was empty. In short, the disciples doubt Mary's word until they see Jesus themselves, and all John has added is that Thomas doubts the disciple's words until he sees Jesus himself.

With that in mind, let us look at the words of Jesus to Thomas. Again and again, many ministers claim that Jesus is reprimanding Thomas' doubt. But is he? Jesus' questioning words to Thomas are profound, "Have you believed because you have seen me? Blessed are those who have not seen and yet have come to believe" (John 20:29). As we already pointed out earlier, these words are not directed only to Thomas. Christ's words bless those who have not needed to "see" to believe, something that Mary required, something which the other disciples required (who doubted Mary), and something that Thomas needed (when he doubted the disciples).

Yet, aside from who it was directed to, what exactly is Jesus' rebuke? It is not, as so many have claimed, a rebuke of doubt itself. Far from it. Jesus never once condemns Thomas or the disciples *because of* doubting, but rather rebukes their personal requirement (stated explicitly by Thomas) to never believe unless they first see. In other words, Jesus accepts doubt's healthy role in our faith, but rejects an unhealthy requirement for the eradication of doubt. His warning is not that doubt is wrong, but that our desire for its removal is! A requirement for certainty, the opposite of doubt, is what Jesus condemns. Ironically, rather than rebuking a skeptical mindset, Jesus actually condemns the need for a faith based on certainty, the sort of faith that so many who condemn Thomas from the pulpit promote.

Jesus implores Thomas to believe. But what exactly does that mean? Biblical scholar Marcus Borg notes that our familiar English word carries a forgotten meaning. "Prior to the seventeenth century," he wrote, "the word 'believe' did not mean believing in the truth of statements or propositions." In fact, "grammatically, the object of believing was not statements, but a person." So what did it mean in English to say that you believed something?

Most simply, "to believe" meant "to love." Indeed, the English words "believe" and "belove" are related. What we believe is what we belove.[2]

We can note something else too: to love something is to trust it. Trust is not the same thing as certainty. Far from it! For example, when I love my wife, I place my trust in her. That does not mean that I can never question anything regarding her, but rather that I am certain that my trust is well placed in her. It means that because of my trust, my doubts are either directed at myself (do I know her as well as I should?) or toward something abnormal in her own actions (why is she acting the opposite of how she normally does?). As such, there is always a careful balance between trust and doubt in any bond. The same is true of our faith and relationship with Jesus. Doubt is a healthy part of our walk with God. We need doubt to help us to evaluate the Bible, to grow deeper in our understanding of Christ, and even to recognize the Holy Spirit (as opposed to any other rival spirit).

Because biblical scholars, theologians, and scientists often deal in matters of doubt, Thomas has sometimes been called the "academic's apostle." While that has a nice ring to it, I would disagree only because I know that doubt is not special to those of us who study in the halls of schools. It is a constant friend or enemy to many in the Christian faith, professional and ordinary alike. The sad reality is that so many have felt and are continued to be made to feel ashamed of such things. Doubt, they hear, is the enemy of faith, when the opposite is true: it is a great ally.

Even before the crucifixion, we find Jesus showing a positive attitude toward those who doubt. For example, take John the Baptist. He is remembered and immortalized at the beginning of every Gospel account as the prophetic voice declaring the way for Jesus' future ministry. He's as much a symbol of true and sure faith as any that can be imagined. And so, it is surprising how few remember that every Gospel account also records that shortly before John's death (beheaded at the request of King Herod's dancing daughter), John came to *doubt* whether Jesus really was the Messiah after all.

> *When John heard in prison what the Messiah was doing, he sent word by his disciples and said to him, "Are you the one who is to come, or are we to wait for another?" Jesus answered them, "Go and tell John what you hear and see: the blind receive their sight, the lame walk, the lepers are cleansed, the deaf hear, the dead are raised, and the poor have good news brought to them..."*

> – MATTHEW 11:2–6

According to the stories, John sent messengers to Jesus asking him (with perhaps a hint of sarcasm), whether he was the promised one or they should continue to wait for another. The last major prophet before Jesus, the one who Jesus himself said there was "no one greater," and who was like Elijah ... *doubted* Jesus' ministry. He *doubted* Christ. And guess what? As theologian Fritz Guy notes: "Jesus did not reject the question as improper, criticize John for a lack of faith, appeal to his own self-authenticating authority, or exhort John to believe." Instead, "Jesus both respected and appealed to John's intelligence and rationality by pointing to evidence."[3] Just like with his disciples, Jesus routinely shows an open and encouraging response to the questions and doubts that are directed toward him. Moreover, in each of these narratives, the people doubting grow in their faith *because* of their doubts.

A HUMBLE FAITH

But some may wonder: how can doubt be a good thing if our faith is built on certainty? The answer: it's not. That's why Jesus, although welcoming Thomas' doubt, discouraged his demand for certainty. Because in truth, our faith is actually built on humility.

> *For we know only in part, and we prophesy only in part; but when the complete comes, the partial will come to an end. When I was a child, I spoke like a child, I thought like a child, I reasoned like a child; when I became an adult, I put an end to childish ways. For now we see in a mirror, dimly, but then we will see face to face. Now I know only in part; then I will know fully, even as I have been fully known.*

– I CORINTHIANS 13:9–12

This is a famous text in Christianity, which makes it all the more surprising that so few actually recognize the curious and slightly unorthodox message that it contains. Paul is speaking *as* a Christian *about* Christians. In other words, he is not saying that "the world" knows only dimly, but we as Christians know in full. He is not saying that we were children before Christ, but have now become adults *in* Christ. No, he isn't saying that at all. Instead, he's describing what Christians are *after* Jesus.

According to Paul, it is *because* of Jesus that we know as much as a child does. *Because* of Jesus, we know only in part. *Because* of Jesus, we now see dimly. So what does that mean about *before* Jesus? It means that before the incarnation of Christ, we knew almost nothing (not even "in part"). Before Jesus, we were blind (we couldn't even see "dimly"). In short, it means that before Jesus, we weren't even born yet!

The great news of Paul in 1 Cor. 13:9–12 is that because of Jesus, we can finally see … something (but not much). Talk about humility! But it's even more humble than you imagine. The Greek word translated as "dimly" isn't what it sounds like in English. The Greek word is αἰνίγματι (*ainigmati*), where we get the word "enigma" from; and it means the same thing as it sounds like: it refers to something that is itself *a riddle*, something indirect, difficult, obscure, and very perplexing. So, Paul literally says in that verse that "now we see an enigma," or to better get the sense: "now we see an obscure perplexing riddle." Crowd stirring, isn't it? And mind you, he's describing the Christian faith.

What does an "obscure perplexing riddle" tell us? Well, it tells us that Paul has a sense that what Jesus revealed was only a small taste of the *real* truth. There is something bigger coming, something so incomprehensible that everything we already think we know is similar to a child imagining there's nothing left to experience in adulthood. Paul is inviting Christians to recognize that far from having all the answers, they are but children beginning the journey. The promise, not the present reality, is that we will eventually meet "face to face."

Jesus, although revealing God in the incarnation, scarcely scratched the surface of the divine. The fact that we often feel as if we received so much light and revelation already, Paul would likely say, is just evidence of how deeply we were in the dark before. Even an obscure and riddling *enigma* seems like a stunning vision of clarity when compared to pitch-black blindness.

So now, maybe we can better understand why Paul urged the church at Thessalonica to "test/question/doubt everything; and keep all that is good." Because at the end of the day, Christianity for Paul was never about claiming to have the answers and reciting them, but was always an admission of humility and the beginning of a search for them, a search Paul likely believed was only now possible thanks to Jesus.

STANDING WITH JESUS

But was Paul crazy? Sure, we've seen the disciples doubt. Yes, we've even seen Paul encourage doubt and undermine any idea that Christianity is a religion built on certainty and clarity. Yet, could they all just be wrong? Could perhaps their doubt simply be evidence of their own blindness? Should we really be drawing these lessons from them? The answer is a resounding yes. Why? Because Jesus did it too.

When it was noon, darkness came over the whole land until three in the afternoon. At three o'clock Jesus cried out with a loud voice, "Eloi, Eloi, lema sabachthani?" which means, "My God, my God, why have

*you forsaken me?" … Then Jesus gave a loud cry and breathed his last.
And the curtain of the temple was torn in two, from top to bottom.*

– MARK 15:33–38

Though often ignored and explained away, Jesus himself is the poster child of doubt in the Gospels of Mark and Matthew. Here, we find a vision of Christ so striking and challenging that it remains haunting for many who read his words. The very epitome of human existence is encapsulated in this one moment by Jesus during his incarnation. It is here that some would argue Jesus demonstrates his true humanity.

Peter Rollins, a philosopher and theologian from Ireland, describes Jesus' cry of doubt as "the true scandal of the cross." What is that scandal? That Jesus experienced an "existential atheism" on Calvary's hill.[4] It is not that Jesus actually stops believing in God (a rational atheism), but rather that Jesus stops sensing God (existential). "On the cross, Christ undergoes the deepest, most radical form of divine loss, one that is experienced." He argues that "it is only when we see the crucifixion as the moment where God loses everything that we begin to glimpse the true theological significance of the event."[5]

In his book *Insurrection*, he writes that:

> *While various religious systems provide a place for this painful experience of unknowing (as a test, as something to endure, or something to overcome), in Christianity when one is crushed by a deep, existential loss of certainty, one finds oneself in Christ … we find the staggering message of the Cross: Radical doubt, suffering, and the sense of divine forsakenness are central aspects of Christ's experience and thus a central part of what it means to participate in Christ's death. The moment we feel the loss of all that once gave us meaning is not a time in which we are set free from Christ, nor is a moment where we fall short of Christ: It is the time when we stand side by side with Christ.*[6]

The subtitle of his book sums up well the implication of this understanding of the cross: "to believe is human, to doubt, divine." Rather than the enemy of faith, Rollins argues that the experience of doubt is the moment in which man and God unite in the most intimate of ways. Anyone can believe an intellectual truth. Or to quote the letter of James: "Even the demons believe!" (James 2:19). Doubting, on the other hand, is something that as far as Scripture witnesses to, only humans and God have ever shared.

Jesus' doubt on the cross sends an important message to all who are willing to listen: if Christ could undergo and experience such deep and piercing doubts, he can relate to your own. If he could doubt God while hanging on the cross, he can sympathize with your own piercing cries as you limp to your own crucifix. As Rob Bell writes in his classic book *Velvet Elvis*, that " ...the kind of faith Jesus invites us into doesn't skirt the big questions ... but takes us deep into the heart of them." Because in the end, there is, after all, "no question that Jesus cannot handle, no discussion too volatile, no issue too dangerous."[7]

And yet, if Jesus can handle any question that we come to him with, then why are so many Christians convinced that there are some questions that aren't acceptable to bring up in church? Why are so many in conservative denominations taught to bury their "doubts"? Why has Paul's vision of stark Christian humility transformed for many into a narcissistic and self-congratulatory pride? People have deep-seated questions and almost nowhere to take them. And this has grave consequences for some. As Austin Fischer, a pastor in Texas, wisely put it: "People don't abandon their faith because they have doubts so much as people abandon their faith because they think they're not allowed to have doubts."[8]

It is an unavoidable truth that we inhabit a post-modern and post-certain world, and many find themselves fighting the forces of skepticism and doubt. Yet, this is a losing battle. For no matter how much one tells you to believe, doubt will not magically disappear unless one is intellectually dishonest. We all cry, just as the father did to Jesus: "I believe! Help my unbelief!" (Mark 9:24). Yet, we mistake the unbelief as a problem to solve rather than a tool to aid us in the Spirit's ministry. Doubt in other words is healthy. Or as biblical scholar Peter Enns writes: "Doubt is sacred."[9]

For far too long, the church has looked at Christians who doubt as either a threat or problem to solve, rather than what they have the potential to be: a blessing. In every church, just as with the disciples in Matthew, we as the body of Christ can report that "some doubted," and just as back then, Jesus still calls and commissions us to move forward not in spite of our doubts but alongside them. In a world and society that revels in its supposedly secular and post-modern age of skepticism, Christianity and Scripture offer untapped treasures for the church, if only it can listen to them and be brave enough to put them to good use.

And so, I want to suggest that if we are to rediscover the power of the Bible and the witness it bears, we must not be afraid to bring our nagging doubts and questions about it to the table. We must trust that Jesus is big enough to handle our "childish" thoughts. If we are to try and slowly grow to be adults (as Paul continually hoped), we must throw everything of ourselves into this endeavor. Moreover, we must recognize and be willing to accept that as Paul himself intimated, we will often find the truth encased and mixed with the false. Growing our faith to adulthood means recognizing that this is as true of Scripture as it is of the world at large.

Excerpt from the book, *Saying No to God: A Radical Approach to Reading the Bible Faithfully*, by Matthew J. Korpman, Quoir Publishing, 2019.

4

WHY DO WE DECONSTRUCT?

MICHELLE COLLINS

John Caputo, in *What Would Jesus Deconstruct*, saw the process of deconstruction in a way that "things are made to tremble by their own inner impulse, by a force that will give them no rest, that keeps forcing itself to the surface, forcing itself out, making the thing resolve." It sounds so mysterious and to some extent it is, but the reality is that there are multiple psychological processes happening at any given moment that fall outside of our conscious thought. It is in those psychological processes that the answers lie as to why we are ignorant of other beliefs or why we just choose to not acknowledge them. Some of this is pretty amazing and actually makes me feel a lot better as it pertains to all the years that I just did not seem awake.

COGNITIVE DISSONANCE, CONFIRMATION BIAS, AND NAÏVE REALISM

Hindsight is 20/20 or so they say.

Everyone seems to understand that in looking back we can ascertain what "really" happened or make better sense of our understanding of a situation. In the middle of a situation though, I wonder how often people stop and ask themselves what is really happening. I mean the first problem with that of course is how do you know you're in the middle of something? And the view from within the situation is far different than the view outside the situation, that is why it is easier to give advice than to receive it.

Looking back on my religious belief experience, I see the holes in understanding. I see the questions and contradictions. Why did I not see them then? I am sure we can all ask ourselves that question about a lot of different subjects, but in the case of something so closely held as a religious belief, how do we not stop, look around, and ask questions? I remember being baptized. I distinctly remember the feelings of so desperately wanting to be baptized. I begged repeatedly only to be told I was not ready. I remember standing in the middle of the sanctuary with my grandmother and asking once again. The pastor was there as well and asked me what baptism meant. I was only a small child, but I knew. I explained it in my child-like understanding and must have presented a good argument as to my understanding because he decided I was ready.

I remember being scared of going under the water (I had a bad experience in a pool at around 4 or 5 years of age) but knowing this was how I showed God my allegiance. Looking back, that was what I was trying to do. I wanted everyone, but most importantly God, to know I was serious about my desired relationship. I guess I had some magic idea in my head about how I would feel after, yet nothing seemed to change except the expectations of those around me and the expectations I placed on myself.

Growing up in a belief system seems like the right thing. I had wandered away from my beliefs for quite a while in early adulthood only to once again look for God when I had my first child. It is interesting how becoming a parent makes you yearn for some kind of certainty. Once you have a child, you set out to raise them up correctly and if you have a strongly held belief, it is that belief with which you will teach your child. Not many will stand by and allow the child to find their own way, it does not seem like good parenting. I was raised in that way and so were my children. So why is it that we never ask questions even when we see problems?

COGNITIVE DISSONANCE

I believe that cognitive dissonance plays a large part in the discussion of belief systems and our inability to see past them. Most have probably heard of the term but have yet to introspectively evaluate its role in their own lives. The short version explanation is psychological stress felt by a person who is confronted with a belief that contradicts their own ideas or values. Regardless of the evidence presented for the new information, the human psyche defends itself from the clash by seeking a reason for the difference, other than just being wrong.

Leon Festinger was a social psychologist that worked in the field studying cognitive dissonance. It is his contention that human beings strive for internal psychological consistency to function mentally in the real world. In other words, we need things to make sense. So, what happens when we are confronted with information that falls outside our paradigm? Well, we begin to sweat, mentally speaking but maybe physically as well. We need to justify our belief or perspective in order to reduce the dissonance. So, how does one reduce this type of mental disquiet? Well, there are several ways. We can change our minds (come on you know most people who disagree with you religiously are so open to changing their minds, give it a try). Okay, maybe not, but what about changing the rules? Or how about just denying the new information as though it doesn't exist? Ok, I am going to throw some psychological jargon at you. Ready?

> *The contradiction of a belief, ideal or system of values, causes cognitive dissonance that can be resolved by changing the challenged belief yet, instead of effecting change, the resultant mental stress restores psychological consonance to the person, by misperception, rejection or refutation of the contradiction, seeking moral support from people who share the contradicted beliefs or acting to persuade other people that the contradiction is unreal"*

Hence a mob if you are familiar with social media. You know how this goes ... you post some new belief or idea that you are contemplating. Rather than discussion or addressing the belief itself, often those responding just simply turn to attacking your character, your background, or just overall ganging up on you to tell you that you are wrong. Rarely will someone engage in actual discussion of the idea itself. You know what I am talking about. We have all had someone tag in their friends or maybe we have done it ourselves. Hmmmm ...

Let's think about this for a moment with an example that happens far too often. Most within Christianity are familiar with end times prophecy. I remember growing up terrified that those around me may just disappear one day and I would be left alone. Strangely, I never seemed to count myself among those that would be raptured ... foreshadowing? Anyway, every little while we are told of a new blood moon, or an impending date arrived at by "serious" study of the bible and some numerology thrown in for fun. It has literally become a running joke in my social media experience each time one of these doomsday predictions goes by without the end happening. You've seen the jokes, "I survived the blood moon of such and such date!" Those that truly are sold on "maybe this time" are sincere in their belief, so what do they do when they are wrong? Most will simply explain away the occurrence as incorrect numerology, misunderstood prophecy, or even God simply giving us another chance. How many actually begin to question the belief itself? And if you are one that does begin to question, you are counted among those that fall away and are apostate. Convenient! What is really amazing is that often these missed prophecies actually strengthen the resolve of those espousing the belief. It's like a novice gambling who doubles down after losing.

CONFIRMATION BIAS

So, what fuels this cognitive dissonance? Are you ready for another term? Confirmation bias ... we all have it to some extent. This is the human tendency to cherry-pick information that looks and sounds like what we already believe. Ironically to the subject, confirmation bias tends to be most pronounced when it involves ingrained, ideological and emotional beliefs, like politics, religion, or sports teams.

Confirmation bias is like reading the end of a book first and then viewing the book and all its contents from that perspective. Everyone wants to know who did it in a mystery. So, you read the end, find out, and then go back to the book for all the details. In reading the details, you pick up on evidence that points to who you already know to be the culprit. You read through a lens. The same thing happens when we continually expose ourselves to certain news sites and channels. We begin to only hear what we already believe. I am sure by this point you are remembering something learned in church that you are sure is true and you have the articles to prove it. But, are those articles the only perspective? Let's go back to the example above regarding end times prophecy.

I grew up hearing of the rapture and the only argument that occurred was whether it was pre-tribulation, mid-tribulation, or post-tribulation. I read everything I could get my hands on about the subject. Hal Lindsey's "Late Great Planet Earth" was dog eared and worn out from all the times I checked it against what was happening in the world via the news channel. Imagine my surprise when one of the first tenets of my religious beliefs that was challenged was this very subject, and I was told that "Futurism" is only one of four perspectives on end-times prophecy. Not so fast, do you want to know the others? They would be historicist, preterist, and idealist. That's all you get. I am not in charge of your journey, so if you are interested, give them a look. Just beware as all views have their defenders who operate in their own confirmation bias.

So, what is the philosophy behind the phenomena of confirmation bias? It goes back to the early Greeks. In *The History of the Peloponnesian War*, Thucydides is credited for saying "For it is a habit of humanity to entrust to careless hope what they long for, and to use sovereign reason to thrust aside what they do not fancy." Now let's be fair, we have come a long way and maybe our brain is just not wired for all the information it receives. Simple is better and learning or understanding complicated subjects is difficult. How many of us have time to evaluate the importance of quantum physics as we go about our day? Now throw in that quantum physics may hold answers to religious questions and the overall instinct is to push it away and call it silly. Is it? Probably not. There is much to learn in the field of science, yet we generally have neither the time nor inclination to explore it. It makes sense in light of this to look for and defend information that supports what we already believe or have learned. We have taken the verse "do not be conformed to this world" to mean that the world must conform to our ideas.

I do not want you to assume that confirmation bias is only a negative thing. In fact, let's dispense with good or bad, it just exists and how it is used determines its value. Let's consider music for a moment. Music is actually mathematical. The number of beats and rests, the flow of the overall piece, and the anticipation of the next beat is all brain science. Our brains adapt to certain genres of music because we almost know what to expect. There is a satisfaction in anticipating the next down beat and then hearing it just as we anticipated. Our brains are conditioned. Good or bad comes from what we condition it with and how stringent we are regarding how we allow our brains to evaluate new knowledge. So, this brings us to the subject of what I am discussing - religious deconstruction. For those that have started down this path, often you will have no reason as to why the process started. As I have already shared, I can think of no one thing that sparked the internal debate, only that it began and has continued regardless of my comfort levels.

NAÏVE REALISM

This brings me to another similar discussion, one on the subject of naïve realism. Naïve realism is the tendency to believe that how we view the world, politics, or even the bible, and religion is the objective reality. We fail to recognize that we have a lens or perspective that taints objective reality thereby making it subjective. Everything that we evaluate is an interpretation of the real thing, even God. No one can know for sure who or what God is, we only have ideas. Peter Rollins is an Irish philosopher, and I absolutely love listening to him. He is so intelligent, and he has a great accent. Anyway, I once heard him say that as soon as you begin to describe God, you diminish him. That is a striking thought, one that makes a great amount of sense. Any description we give to God is only able to come from a place of our experience or desire. This becomes problematic in the face of naïve realism. "People's beliefs and perceptions are a function of both the objective properties of the world and the psychological processes that translate those objective features into psychologically experienced features." Even those aware of this phenomenon and take corrective action still are often unaware of just how short they fall in their estimation. We give ourselves a large amount of room in our self-evaluation.

Another expectation within naïve realism is that our beliefs and thoughts are realistic, so it follows that if other people are reasonable, they will come to the same conclusions. It is a projection of our own desires, beliefs, and feelings onto others. Of course, those that share our obvious understanding are considered allies or friends, but those that counter with differing ideas become unreasonable in our minds. Now apply this to political and religious ideas. It is easy to see why we end up so at odds with one another to the point of ad hominin comments, unattractive labels, and downright unchristian like attitudes toward others, all because they refuse to believe like we do.

CONSTRUCTIVE ALTERNATIVISM

I know, I know … I have thrown a lot of psychological jargon at you so far but let's add a little more, so your brain sufficiently hurts. In an effort to reduce uncertainty, science is constantly evaluating ideas for value and objectivity as it pertains to the outcomes. The scientific method of systematic observation, measurement, and experimentation sets the tone for a conclusion. Science and those who work within its realm usually do not have a problem admitting that there is much they do not know, hence the need for continual hypothesis, experimentation, and changing outcomes.

George Kelly was a humanistic psychologist who observed that while the goal of science was to reduce uncertainty, everyday human beings had the same desire. We all like our certainty and it is one of our foundational needs. So, while science creates system and experimentation, human beings create constructs. The goal of both is to postulate something and prove its trustworthiness. Constructive alternativism is born! For Kelly, the enjoyment of an experience is not the important part, it is whether our outcomes validate our predictions. In other words, people are free to come to their own conclusions based on the constructs they use. As an event can be interpreted in numerous ways, the truth of the event is less important than finding those that seem to interpret in the same way. Allies!

It is not the shared background of a religious understanding as much as it is the construct that is used to evaluate like-mindedness. What do I mean by that? Well, thousands of people claim the same religious construct, but their backgrounds and personalities are not necessarily similar. As such, the construct is their common ground. Out of all the belief systems out there, they have chosen this construct, found their allies, and see the world from this perspective only. Changing this means that the construct itself must be questioned. Now my head hurts!

HERBART'S APPERCEPTIVE MASS

Have you ever had a moment of déjà vu? You know, that feeling that you have done the exact same thing or been in the exact same place before. This happens to me a lot and there are many theories as to why: a glitch in the matrix, neurological disorders, prophetic gifting, and I am sure many others. Somewhere along the way in this journey I began to ponder the opposite. Why had so many of my questions never occurred to me before. I mean some of them seem so obvious to me now, so where was I all that time. I have often compared the experience to being asleep only to wake up where I am currently with all this newfound knowledge. Even better, have you ever been driving only to realize that you arrived somewhere without remembering how you did so? We are so inclined to muscle memory that we just function without a lot of thought sometimes. But this feels different.

For years, I was involved in bible reading, communion, religious study, and all the activities that make up the religious experience. Yet, nowhere along the way did I stop to evaluate what I was learning or what I believed. I just functioned without a lot of thought. I called it faith; I am sure others would not identify it that way.

I have often stopped along the way now to berate myself for missing such obvious things. I seemingly want to kick myself for never asking why. Not too long ago in the course of my psychological study, I came across an early psychologist and his theory of apperceptive mass. Okay, no glossing over, this is important! Johann Friedrich Herbart was an early philosophical and educational student in the late 1700s to early 1800s. His interests included mathematical application to psychology. As such, and without going into a lot of dusty background, he developed something called psychic mechanics. He believed that ideas had the power to either attract or repel other ideas, depending upon compatibility.

According to Herbart, ideas actually compete with one another to find place within the consciousness. Starting to make sense? As you can imagine, this seemingly puts the mind as a battleground for expression. No idea ever goes away, it just seeks to find its place in the conscious and until such a time, exists in the subconscious.

When ideas battle with one another, those that "lose" do not disappear, they just lose some of their intensity and sink into the subconscious. Confused yet?

Think back to your experience of junior high school for a moment. Remember how you were part of a group. For some it was the popular kids, for others the athletes, and for many of us outcasts, but we had each other. Generations have grown up on this idea in movies, and it strikes a chord within us for the underdogs. Okay, now let's apply this same idea to that of our ideas and conscious mind.

Herbart postulated that groups of compatible ideas exist together within the consciousness. He referred to this as an apperceptive mass. Basically, it is all the ideas to which we give our attention. When new ideas occur, they must be compatible with the apperceptive mass in order for us to give it our attention. It is absolutely fascinating. So, let's go back to junior high school for a moment and imagine that all the popular kids are standing together in a group doing what they do. Along comes a new student who looks a certain way, acts a certain way, and is seeking admittance into the group. If that new student is compatible with the group, he or she will be accepted and absorbed. If, however, there is no compatibility, the group will work in concert to repel the interloper.

Herbart expresses this expulsion as repression. The idea does not go away as we have already discussed, but it sinks into obscurity and bides its time. Now imagine that enough of these rejected students end up grouped together. It will not be long before they challenge the power structure for control of the playground. This is where we all cheer and identify with this group in the movies. The underdog gets the girl, the geek wins class president, the new heretical idea gets its day in the sun. Eventually, the repressed ideas will challenge the status quo and force their way into the conscious thought. Voila!

It sounds so simple and yet it obviously is not. This process takes time, maybe even years. I am convinced that this is the answer to my question pertaining to how I could have missed these obvious questions for so long. I did not miss them, they just took time to find their place alongside other new ideas.

THE CORRELATION OF COGNITIVE DISSONANCE AND GRIEF

So, as I have already mentioned, grief is subjective as is the deconstructive process. It is not my place to tell anyone when they have finished grieving or deconstructing. However, one of the issues as it pertains to deconstruction is the idea of rushing the process. That can happen whether grieving a death or intimate life change. Understandably, we want to move past the pain. The problems begin when we force ourselves to move on without examining or experiencing the emotions that are natural to the process. When I first stumbled into this process, I just wanted to feel happy again. In speaking with those who I supposed were ahead of me in the process, I heard things such as "five years ago when this all began" or "I haven't prayed or read my bible in years," I panicked. How would I survive these feelings for that long? How would I ever be a functioning human being again? Would God wait for me? Was I capable of this and did I even get a choice in the matter? In hindsight, these questions all seem normal now but then all I could do was panic and feel out of control.

Part of the problem is that we still see this process as linear. I question this tenet, then the next, and the next, and so on. That is not how this works. That is not how any of this works! Grieving our ideals and beliefs, and in some cases even God, is not a neat little project upon which we embark with the finish line firmly in our sights. This is a dark, emotional, and in some cases, disastrous event. So, our minds attempt to protect us from the loss and heartbreak by seeking out a reason, and voilà … cognitive dissonance. We convince ourselves somewhere along the way that we are at the supposed finish line, so when those very real emotions show up again, there is a sense of confusion. We end up blaming the confusion on something else or maybe something we ate the night before.

There was a school of thought within the history of psychology called stoicism. Basically, this ideal is the endurance of pain without expressing emotion. This school of thought taught that the highest good is based on knowledge and that we should be indifferent to pleasure and pain. It is a means of self-control that is often present within those expressing grief. Often, we will put on a happy face, make new relationship connections, and carry on with life. Sitting somewhere in the background are all these unresolved emotions and questions. It would be shortsighted to assume you can move forward with no repercussions. Our emotions always come out, and sometimes in ways in which we wished they did not.

I spoke with an individual who had questioned God and some of the basic tenets of Christianity. They felt sure they had dealt with their emotions and in an effort to return to "normal" found a new church and jumped in with both feet. Every time the emotions would come up and the questions would return, only to be suppressed, convincing themselves that they had already traversed this path and had no reason to return. Interestingly enough, they even wrote a book on their experience in which there was a happy ending, a return to God and church. So, what was the problem?

The absolute breakdown emotionally in the middle of a church service. Out of nowhere, they found themselves reacting to a statement from the pulpit and they could not stop the cascade of emotion and word vomit that ensued. They found themselves on their feet, yelling that none of it is true. God does not exist and if he did, he was a cruel bastard that had no concern for his creation. Dramatic pause …

So, what happened here? How many of us have felt something along these lines and found ourselves in a conversation in which we were suddenly angry or sad when we thought everything was okay. Of course, most of us do not have this experience, although I will be honest and say that part of the reason that I still will not return to church is because I am afraid of something like this happening. I have an expressive face and roll my eyes a lot when I hear things that I consider bull … you get the point! We can only convince ourselves that all is okay for so long. In the end, the process wins, it gets its way and we are merely along for the ride. Grief will make its way out whether we choose to recognize it or not.

Excerpt from the book, *Into The Gray: The Mental and Emotional Aftermath of Spiritual Deconstruction*, by Michelle Collins, Quoir Publishing 2021.

5

BEAUTY IN THE WRECKAGE

BRANDON ANDRESS

I have heard many people say over the years that our lives are like icebergs. In fact, my brother-in-law has a tattoo of an iceberg on his forearm, which reminds me of this premise every time I see him. His tattoo is accompanied with the words, "I am not an island. I am an iceberg." The implication being that there is so much more to him than what you see on the surface. There is a depth below the surface that many people may not even realize.

To me, the image of an iceberg is so evocative. There is this massive, colossal behemoth, floating in the water, of which only ten percent is ever visible to the naked eye, while the other ninety percent remains hidden or unseen. Like each of our lives.

There is so much more below the surface of one's life, so much more at the depths of one's being, than anything we will ever see on the surface. And this may be true for you at this exact moment.

You may be trying your best to put a smile on your face and hold it together when you are around other people. You may be trying to pull up your bootstraps each morning and keep your routine so that you don't draw the attention of family and friends. You may be trying to do your very best to look composed in front of everyone who sees you, as if everything is okay in your life. But down deep in your heart and soul, below the surface where no one else can see, you are aching.

Maybe you have lost a child, a parent, a friend, or a pet this year. Maybe you have been diagnosed with a terminal illness or know someone who has been. Maybe you are dealing with and carrying regret for relationships that have been destroyed because of your words or actions. Maybe you are lost and alone and don't have anyone standing next to you, holding you up, or giving you the strength to carry on. Maybe you are holding on to disappointments and failures and wondering if you have any worth, value, or dignity remaining. Maybe you have had a miscarriage or had difficulty getting pregnant. Maybe you have lost a job, hate your job, and are struggling to provide or find a new way forward. Maybe you have reached the height of success but still feel empty inside and without purpose. Maybe you have hurt your friends and your family and you feel as if you can never be forgiven. Maybe your marriage is on the rocks, or in complete shambles, and you just don't know how, or if, the pieces can ever be put back together.

Maybe, maybe, maybe.

Somehow there has been this unrealistic idea invented within many faith communities, either intentionally or unintentionally, that living in our sufferings and carrying a broken heart is incompatible with experiencing life transformation or living a full, abundant life. We have been led to believe that it is an either/or proposition, because there is no way a person can be transformed by the Spirit, used by God, or experience an abundant and overflowing life presently while still carrying our pain.

That is absolutely not true.

Even though we presently ache and groan from the wreckage around us and as we carry our wounded and broken hearts with us, it is still possible to enter the sweet embrace of heaven and earth, to experience the perfect freedom and perfect love of God, and discover joy and an abundant life.

I know this may sound impossible or contradictory to what you have ever been taught or told in your church, but it's the absolute truth.

Likely the most influential biblical passage for me over the last decade comes from the letter written by Paul to the church in Rome. It is an astonishingly beautiful passage in the way he describes the difficulty and pain of this present life, while also detailing a creation that is pregnant with new life and hope.

All around us we observe a pregnant creation. The difficult times of pain throughout the world are simply birth pangs. But it's not only around us; it's within us. The Spirit of God is arousing us within. We're also feeling the birth pangs. These sterile and barren bodies of ours are yearning for full deliverance. That is why waiting does not diminish us, any more than waiting diminishes a pregnant mother. We are enlarged in the waiting. We, of course, don't see what is enlarging us. But the longer we wait, the larger we become, and the more joyful our expectancy.

Meanwhile, the moment we get tired in the waiting, God's Spirit is right alongside helping us along. If we don't know how or what to pray, it doesn't matter. The Spirit does our praying in and for us, making prayer out of our wordless sighs, our aching groans.

The Spirit knows us far better than we know ourselves, knows our pregnant condition, and keeps us present before God. That's why we can be so sure that every detail in our lives of love for God is worked into something good (1 Romans 8: 22-28).

Right in the middle of the wreckage and pain and suffering that is all around us, and that we presently carry within us, a new life of shalom has been conceived and is growing within each one of us. This new life is growing as we eagerly and expectantly and joyfully anticipate the birth of new creation in fullness in the future. So while we hold together the tension of our pain and our new life of shalom within us, we look forward in hope to a time when all will be made right. But we hold these two things together presently.

It is like a mother who experiences the increasingly intense and powerful pains of pregnancy for nine months leading up to the birth of her baby, yet who is infinitely, immeasurably, inexhaustibly joyful in her anticipation. In the same way, we literally hold within us the tension of our groaning, our pain, and our suffering together with a new life that has been birthed within us.

And we are presently, expectantly, and longingly joyful. That for which we hope to arrive in its fullness one day is within us right now. And it is holding us in our heartache. It is groaning with us in our suffering. It is praying for us in our weakness. And it keeps us in the presence and communion of the Divine even when we feel like we are at our end.

That is why I would encourage you to never give up no matter how difficult life may get. That is why I would encourage you to never stop believing that there is so much good left in this life. That is why I would encourage you to never believe the lies that your pain and suffering has to remain an end destination of your life, or that the only way forward is to leave your broken heart behind, or that you should feel guilty experiencing happiness or joy while carrying your broken heart with you.

I felt this tension powerfully at the end of October in 2017. I received a heartbreaking text message from my work partner, whom I had been partners with for eight years, telling me that she had one to two months to live. She was a breast cancer survivor and had been cancer-free for the last five years. And inexplicably, it came back with a vengeance, in her lungs, liver, and brain. I came home and sat on my back porch and cried. Tears streamed down my face. I was heartbroken.

But as I looked up, I saw my six-year old little boy, Will, with his full Spiderman costume on, running around the yard, jumping and landing like Spiderman, and then pretending to shoot his web. It was the funniest thing to see him playing by himself and using his imagination and having so much fun.

Even with the pain and heartache of that moment, there was still so much beauty and joy. I sat there with a smile and many tears, holding the tension of the two.

We do not have to feel guilty for holding this tension. We can hold and carry our pain and suffering with us while bearing witness to all that is good in this life.

OUR WORST DAY

I know that my words can often drift so far into poetic imagery and theological proof-texting that it may feel as if I have abandoned a real and raw practicality for an unrealistic idealism. But like the mighty and colossal iceberg, there is always so much more below the surface that you can't see. My words on these pages are just the tip of the iceberg that rises above the surface of the water that you can see clearly. But below the surface, in the depths where no one can see, is my own broken heart.

While the last year has been difficult for my family and friends, on so many fronts, nothing could have prepared us for what happened one night in late February of last year.

My house church is a group of my best and closest friends who have gathered together in our home for the last twelve years. On any given Monday evening our house is packed with twelve adults and fifteen kids, three of them now in college, ranging in age from a newborn to twenty years old. We are one big family that has been through the highest highs and the lowest lows together. And the love we have for one another has been strengthened through every single experience we have shared. I love my friends with all of my heart.

It's not uncommon for us to have a text message thread constantly running that includes almost everyone in our group. Many times our messages are about what food someone is bringing when we gather together, crazy emojis or GIFs to celebrate a birthday or a special occasion, or sharing about someone who needs prayer. It gets crazier than that (boom), but you get the general idea.

One Saturday night I sent a text to the group discussing plans for a massive celebration and feast that we would be having on the upcoming Monday. We had been doing a 13-week study on 1st Corinthians, that had actually taken 70-weeks to finish (more on this in Chapter 9), and we were ready to let our hair down and have a serious blowout. But within minutes of my initial text to everyone, the message thread would be completely turned upside-down. We received a text from Jackie about Abbott, her fifteen-year old son. He was being life-lined to a hospital in Indianapolis due to a tragic accident.

I can't even begin to explain how everything changed for each one of us in that moment. Abbott and two of his good friends had just finished playing basketball on an unseasonably warm, early Spring evening. As they left the park and drove for a few miles, they decided to pull over on a side street a couple of miles from the courts to dry off and change clothes. The details of what happened next are not essential for this story, but in the next few moments after the boy's pulled over to change clothes, two of the boys got back in the vehicle and accidentally ran over Abbott.

We were with Adam, Jackie, and their daughter Ella at the trauma center when the trauma team came into the room and told us the news that they could not save Abbott.

It was the worst day of our lives.

There are no words.

There are simply no words.

We stayed at the hospital for hours that felt like years and then ended up at Adam and Jackie's home early the next morning. Family and friends began to arrive carrying both food and broken hearts. And it wasn't just Adam and Jackie's friends and family that showed up at their home. It was all of Abbott's friends as well. They came by the carload.

While it was amazing to see all of these students arriving at the house that February morning, there was something else happening that was even more unimaginable. As the kids came into the house, Adam and Jackie told them to let Abbott's two best friends, who were with him on that fateful Saturday night, know that they, too, were welcome to come to their home.

And it wasn't long before each boy showed up.

It was both the most heart-wrenching and beautiful thing I have ever seen in my life. The boys cried as the came into house and said, "I am sorry. I am sorry. I am so sorry."

Without a single moment of hesitation or judgment or animosity, Adam and Jackie embraced each boy and held them in grace and mercy and forgiveness and said, "It was an accident. Abbott loved you. And we love you."

In my four decades of living, I have never seen the love of Christ more sacrificially demonstrated than in those moments. I stood there with tears streaming down my face.

They were tears of grief and pain. They were tears of profound sadness for Adam, Jackie and Ella. They were tears of profound empathy for Abbott's friends.

But they were also tears of God's overwhelming and fully enveloping love that held Adam and Jackie and that was expressed through them as they held each boy in that moment.

A person could hear a thousand sermons, spend a lifetime studying the Bible, and yet never see the sweet embrace of heaven and earth, the enveloping and all-consuming love of God, so clearly, so perfectly embodied as it was in my dear friends in that moment.

Amid the horrific and unimaginable tragedy, the earth-shattering heartache, the devastation of complete wreckage, there was a beauty that defied all logic, that defied every human sensibility.

And every single person in that place on that day was a witness to it. We felt it holding us. It was sustaining us in our utter brokenness. And that indescribable beauty, that glorious beauty, surrounded every one of us. But it was because of Adam and Jackie, even in their incomprehensible, unimaginable pain and suffering, that this magnificent beauty was welcomed into that place, at that moment.

And it is specifically because of how they chose to bless when it would have been easier to curse, of how they chose to forgive when it would have been easier to blame, of how they chose to love when it would have been easier to hate that we still see the concentric waves of that beauty washing over us more than a year later.

But the pain of that fateful day still feels like it was yesterday. It's not as if a turn of the calendar page erases the heaviness of a heart, or takes away the burdened weight that one carries. It's not even as if the welcoming of a new year can reset your mind or help you forget the previous.

The days come and go.

The weeks accumulate.

Yet the heartache remains.

Our groaning does not understand time.

Our pain does not end with the calendar year.

Our suffering does not dissipate with the passing days.

It is real yesterday, today, and tomorrow. It is here and here and here, moment by moment, and has no regard for imaginary and illusory divisions of time, nor does it wane with the opening of gifts or with yuletide cheer, nor is it convinced to subside with New Year's resolutions.

Our groaning, our pain, our suffering has no regard for hours, days, weeks, months, years, centuries, or millennia. We carry it with us everywhere we go.

So, while we may have been witnesses to indescribable beauty, to a moment when heaven and earth literally came together, right in the middle of so much pain and suffering, and even while we still feel the waves of it washing over us, is it even possible to believe that we can enter into the shalom of the Divine while we still hurt? Is it even possible to believe that we can experience life to the fullest, life in all of its abundance, not just in fleeting moments, but each moment of the day while still carrying this heartache? Is it too unrealistic to believe that there is any more beauty to discover and receive in this wreckage?

IS JOY AN IMPOSSIBILITY?

I sent a text to Jackie and asked her those same questions before they left as a family for a camping trip to Arkansas during Thanksgiving.

She said that she would need some time think about the questions and that she would take some notes while they were gone.

Here is what she gave to me on a piece of paper a few weeks later:

Losing my son has made me feel the biggest, darkest, most searing pain I have ever experienced in my lifetime. It is an unfathomable black hole. The pain does not dissipate on a daily basis. It is still there. But it hides in little nooks and crannies. It shows up when least expected. And when it does, it literally feels like a huge, gaping hole is being pulled from my chest, right at my heart center. My breath leaves my being and it takes everything I have to find it again. The pain creeps through my body and it wells up through my throat and to my head. There is nowhere for this pain to go. Sometimes it seeps out of my eyes and I have a good cleansing cry. Sometimes the pain turns to anger and I get extremely mad that I no longer have him with me, in the physical. Sometimes the pain turns into an extreme darkness, sadness. This is a place where I can not cry. Wishing I could. Willing myself to do so. This is the place where I want to hide in my own head in distraction.

I have to explain this extreme pain before I can explain the beauty I have seen and felt ever since our tragedy. There are so many moments and I won't be able to explain them all. But there are moments of pure comfort. I can feel Abbott's presence, and it is beautiful, and comforting. I have to quiet my mind for only a short time and I know he is here with me.

Before Abbott was gone, but while we were at the hospital, waiting to hear the terrible news, our family came. And I am not talking about my immediate family. We have the closest Divine-given family, whom we have already been through hell with, and we didn't know they would be with us at 11pm that night, an hour away from home. But during this dark moment, where time is still and all you have is prayer, I looked up and here they came walking toward us. I know this may sound weird, but there was an inexplicable feeling. The way they were walking toward us, together banded-in-arms. They looked like troops, the kind that fight for all that is good. This was the first most beautiful experience. And they haven't left our side all of these months. They continue to lift us and carry us.

Our friends have shared their hearts with us. People we have never met have sent letters, texts, hugs, and encouragement. We have even shared tears with them.

The outpouring of love comes from every direction. We feel as if we are being carried in arms we can't see. I still hear children say prayers for us and Abbott. I see teenagers show huge signs of love. I can be such a cynic of human behavior, but this is just the outer edge of how amazing people have been to us.

Then there are the signs from God proving he is with us, that he is with me. The simplicity of being in nature and feeling the warmth of the sun on my face, on my back. The quiet in the mountains, the rustling of leaves in the trees. The breeze in the air meeting the wind chimes. The richness of the earth. The colors. The smells. The laughter of my daughter. The embrace of my husband. I just have to stop to notice it.

There is a stark contrast between the pain and the beauty of this life. I have to know when to stop looking in the mirror so I can see outside myself. When I turn my attention away from me, the beauty is so evident.

There is a beauty that pierces through the thin veil where heaven and earth come together. It is a present taste of that which will be fully and completely realized in the future. And when we enter into that space, it is an awakening to the resident goodness of all things. It is shalom. It is the experience of pure joy. You can see it. You can feel it.

You can hear it. You can taste it. And you know it is good. And you long for it, not in fleeting, transient moments, but in perpetuity, even when carrying immense pain, even in our suffering.

It is sitting down for that first cup of coffee in the morning, smelling it, tasting it, savoring it. It is every delicate cut of the onion, celery, carrots and the deeply satisfying aroma of the earthy spices when making soup in the cold of winter while the delicate snowflakes fall outside and the fire's warmth radiates around you. It is walking outside on an autumn evening when you close your eyes and breathe deep the magnificent fall fragrance. It is closing your eyes while being enveloped and suspended by your favorite song, noticing every harmony, every note, every melody. It is sitting around a table with your best friends with great food getting lost in conversation. It is holding your baby, hugging your children, the touch of your spouse, and the embrace of your mom and dad while you get lost in the moment. It is a loving church community surrounding parents who just lost their baby. It is watching your son run around the yard in his Spiderman costume and shoot webs. It is embracing and holding two teenage boys in grace and forgiveness and unconditional love.

And it is remembering every good and perfect moment and longing for them once again.

That is shalom invading this broken place. That is the experience of pure joy while carrying our pain. That is the beginning point of learning to see beauty in the wreckage.

That is the ever-present gift of now, an eternal present receiving that we can embody and experience despite our changing life conditions or our painful sufferings.

But it is also the deepest unsatisfied longing of our souls.

We presently receive, but expectantly and longingly anticipate.

Every feeling, every touch, every song, every embrace, every memory, every unsatisfied longing will be satisfied one day. Every terrible wrong will be made right. Every deep wound will be healed. Every crushing heartache will be comforted. Every painful tear will be wiped away.

It is, and it will be, a great joy for all the people.

That for which we hope to arrive in its fullness one day is within us right now. It is embracing us in our heartache. It is groaning with us in our suffering. It is praying for us in our weakness. And holding this tension within us presently is a testament to our faith, not evidence that we lack faith.

Do not let anyone tell you otherwise.

Excerpt from the book, *Beauty In The Wreckage: Finding Peace in the Age of Outrage*, by Brandon Andress, Quoir Publishing, 2018.

6

READING SCRIPTURE THROUGH THE LENS OF CHRIST

KEITH GILES

"Human beings are 'God-breathed,' yet nobody claims we are 'inerrant.' Yet, somehow the Bible we wrote is both?"

— **Matthew Distefano**

Jesus is our key to understanding who God is, what God is like and how we should read the Old Testament scriptures.

This is how the New Testament authors, and even Jesus Himself, defines what it means when we refer to Christ as the "Word of God."

Jesus begins His ministry by teaching His disciples from the Sermon on the Mount where He quite boldly contrasted His teachings with the teachings of Moses, saying:

> *"You have heard that it was said … but I say to you …"*

– MATTHEW 5:38

Try to understand how radical it would be if someone came to your church and said, *"You have heard someone say 'Love one another as I have loved you', but I say to you 'Just love people who love you in return.'"*

Hopefully there would be a huge gasp from the congregation at the audacity of this person to stand up in front of everyone and contradict the words of Jesus. Who does he think he is? What authority does he have to correct the teachings of Christ?

But this is exactly the same kind of statement that Jesus makes when He quotes from Moses and then corrects that teaching with one of His own.

This is also why the people are astonished and whisper to one another at the end of His Sermon about the way He taught.

> *And when Jesus finished these sayings, the crowds were astonished at his teaching, for he was teaching them as one who had authority, and not as their scribes.*

– MATTHEW 7:28–29

Indeed, the authority that Jesus taught with was impressive. He corrected the words of Moses and gave new and more stringent conditions for entering the Kingdom of God, even suggesting that his disciples needed to have a righteousness that surpassed the Pharisees.

This is significant, because it points out what we have already learned from Hebrews 1:1-3, that, at one time, God spoke to us through prophets, but now He has spoken to us through His own Son.

And still today God speaks to us—not merely through the Bible—but through His own Son. Jesus is what God is saying to us in these last days. In the past He spoke to us through the Old Testament, but now, God's message to us is found in Christ.

Remember, Jesus promised us that He would speak to us and that we could hear His voice. Remember that Jesus promised to send us the Holy Spirit who would live within us and would lead us into all truth.

He even said that it was *better for us* that He went away so that He could send us the Spirit who could abide within us and teach us the Words of God, which He would write on our hearts.

Remember also that we have one mediator between God and us and that this mediator is Christ.

> *For there is one God and one mediator between God and mankind, the man Christ Jesus...*
>
> – 1 Timothy 2:5

Our mediator is Christ. Not your pastor. Not your church. Not your denomination. Not your bishops, or elders, or deacons. Only Jesus is our mediator. Only Jesus stands between you and God. Only Jesus connects you to God. Only Jesus reveals who the Father is, and what the Father is like.

So, no one—and nothing—else is stands between you and God. Not even the Bible.

This is what the Bible teaches us: Jesus is our mediator and Jesus is alive within us and we can hear His voice.

We are also told by Jesus Himself that we have one instructor. Who is it?

> *For you have one instructor—the Messiah.*
>
> – Matthew 23:10

Jesus is our instructor. He teaches us. He leads us into all Truth by His indwelling Holy Spirit.

Jesus tells us that He is the Way, and the Truth and the Life (John 14:6).

This means that any scriptures that do not align with what has been revealed to us in Christ are not the whole Truth.

This is our mandate now, from Moses and even from God the Father Himself—"Listen to Jesus!"

This means we need to read the Bible through the lens of Christ if we ever hope to know who God is and what God is really like.

Why else would Paul tell us that *"to this day a veil covers [our] eyes whenever the Old Testament scriptures are read and only in Christ is it taken away"* if this were not the case? (See 2. Cor. 3:14)

Because, without Christ as our lens, or filter, we cannot properly understand what is truth and what is error. But now that we have seen and known Jesus, we truly "see the Father" and we recognize the "Truth" when we see it because Jesus has shown us the "Way" to see the Father clearly.

Therefore, nothing is true unless it lines up with the revelation of Christ. Nothing points the way to God unless it aligns with the teachings of Jesus. Nothing contains the words of life unless those words correspond to the words spoken by Jesus.

As Peter exclaimed:

> *Where else can we go, Lord? You have the words of life.*

> – John 6:68

And as Jesus reminded us:

> *You search the scriptures because you think that in them you have eternal life; and yet you refuse to come to me that you may have life.*

> – John 4:39-40

And as John tells us:

> *"He who has the Son has life, but he who does not have the Son of God does not have life.*

> – 1 John 5:12

In the same way that without Christ we have no life, it could be said that without Christ we have no truth about God either. His unique access to the Father was one of the central claims of His Messianic ministry, as we have already referenced here.

Jesus is the Father's preferred method of speaking to us in these last days. Not through prophets or teachers, not even through apostles or pastors, but through His Son.

Does this mean we should ignore those prophets, teachers, apostles and pastors? Of course not. But what it does mean is that if those prophets, teachers, apostles and pastors say something about God that disagrees with what Jesus has already told us or revealed to us, we must hold tight to the teachings of Christ.

For many, this is where they warn us about being deceived, or remind us how easy it is to fall into error. As if our best and only safeguard against error or deception is to be found in the security of holy men rather than in the absolute authority of Christ and His Holy Spirit that lives within us.

Let us not fool ourselves. These fear-based warnings are more about a desire to maintain control over people in the Church—to ensure they don't question the doctrines of the denomination or challenge the teaching of the pastor in the pulpit.

This is why you will never hear sermons about the priesthood of all believers, or the passages about how the average Christian is capable of hearing the voice of God apart from the approved mediators. To empower the people of God in this way is to effectively dismantle the clergy class and calls into question the entire status quo of traditional Christianity which is built upon coercion and control.

So, we are told to question our ability to hear God's voice. We are told to doubt that still small voice. We're warned not to trust our own discernment. All of this keeps the Holy Spirit of God at a safe distance from the people, only to be handled by the trained professionals in the seminaries. It also, ironically, contradicts the scriptures.

As some New Testament scholars have observed:

We came up with the idea of inerrancy because we needed another mediator between God and man other than Jesus.

– T.F. TORRANCE[53]

It's a very Western certainty. I mean, we don't even have the original manuscripts in order to create [or justify] a certainty out of, yet we've come up with a doctrine that we can be certain of rather than a relationship that we can be certain of ... So, what are we putting our certainty in: the character and nature of a God we are in relationship with, or the certainty of hermeneutical extrapolation that is without encounter?

– WILLIAM PAUL YOUNG[54]

How do you know if your own church community has bought into this fear of the Holy Spirit? It's simple enough to determine. Just try to start a Bible study in your own home and invite some of your friends. See how long it takes for someone to question your ability to lead such a study by yourself. See if anyone demands to see your notes or expects you to ask permission from the leadership first.

I experienced something like this at a church I was serving at over a decade ago. A few college students wanted to start a Bible study in their dorm room with some friends. They were told they could not host this study without one of the pastors leading it, and so they cancelled it.

This astounded me. How could we refuse to allow these twenty-something students to gather and read the words of Jesus together? It was their decision. It was their dorm room. What right did any-one have to tell them they were not qualified to handle the words of Jesus without a professional clergy in the room with them?

53. As quoted by William Paul Young in this video: https://www.youtube.com/watch?v=R BSqUsdClYo&feature=share

54. Ibid.

We often act as if the Gospel and the Scriptures are too danger-ous to be handled by mere mortals. As if the most likely outcome of allowing everyday people to read the Bible would result in confu-sion and false doctrine, not wisdom, insight and freedom.

Let's look at what the New Testament says about all of this:

> *I myself am convinced, my brethren, that you yourselves are full of goodness, complete in knowledge and competent to instruct one another.*
>
> – ROMANS 15:14

> *For you can all prophesy in turn so that everyone may be instructed and encouraged.*
>
> – 1 CORINTHIANS 14:31

What I find fascinating is that, according to Jesus and the Apostles, every believer is capable of hearing the voice of God, and yet, in today's modern church we typically find that only one, or perhaps a few, are expected to hear God's voice and communicate His will to the Body.

Why is that? Partly because we have embraced a false Clergy-Laity divide which suggests that only those who have attended seminary or graduated from Bible College are capable of hearing God's voice or instructing the Body.

As one New Testament scholar, Howard Snyder, put it:

> *The clergy-laity dichotomy is … a throwback to the Old Testament priesthood. It is one of the principal obstacles to the church effectively being God's agent of the kingdom today because it creates a false idea that only 'holy men,' namely, ordained ministers, are really qualified and responsible for leadership and significant ministry. In the New Testament there are functional distinctions between various kinds of ministries but no hierarchical division between clergy and laity. The New Testament teaches us that the church is a community in which all are gifted and all have ministry.*[55]

55. Howard Snyder, *Christ's Body: The Community of the King*, pp.94-95.

Essentially, in spite of the fact that the veil in the temple was torn in two when Christ said "it is finished," we have virtually re-sewn the veil and re-instituted our own system of professional priesthood.

I would like to suggest that it is time for another reformation within the Body of Christ. One where we demolish the clergy-laity distinctions and empower every member to listen for the still, small voice of God.

It's also very important for us to spend time reading the words of Jesus ourselves. This process isn't accomplished in a vacuum. We need to know what Jesus says and we need to become familiar with what He taught. How else can we call ourselves His followers? How can we possibly do what He says if we don't know what He said?

This doesn't mean that everyone has the gift of teaching. We still need to rely on one another and trust the Spirit of Christ that is alive in our community of faith to lead us. We need to pray for, and start to develop our gift of discernment. We need to test the Spirits and hold tightly to the words of Jesus, trusting in His Spirit to guide us.

Everyone who is under the care of the Great Shepherd can hear Him speak. We need to learn to trust Him to do that, and we need to learn to trust ourselves—and especially His Spirit within us—to discern His voice.

Like any skill, this may take time to develop. But if we never step outside our comfort zones and move deeper into an intimate rela-tionship with Jesus, we'll never learn to recognize when He speaks.

What we often forget is that learning and teaching in the Body of Christ isn't merely an academic process. It's not the same as tak-ing a class on Trigonometry or how to speak Chinese. In those cases, it is necessary to have a teacher—an expert in the field—who fully understands the material and has an ability to communicate the necessary information to everyone else. But in the Church, we are not only gathering to understand information about God, are we? Instead, when we gather together the author Himself is always in the room with us. The main character is close at hand to answer any questions and explain everything to us.

For where two or three come together in my name, there am I with them.

– MATTHEW 18:20

If any of you lacks wisdom, he should ask God, who gives generously to all without finding fault, and it will be given to him.

– JAMES 1:5

Can I give you a personal testimony of how God spoke to my wife, Wendy and I at a time when we lacked wisdom?

Around 9:45 p.m. one Sunday night, our doorbell rang. On our doorstep was one of our neighbors standing with her arm around a teenage girl who had a cut over her eye which was bleeding slightly. The girl's name was Angelica. She had just run away from a girl's home which was a few blocks away from where we lived. Angelica had broken through a screened window and tripped on the curb outside in her escape, which is how she had cut her face. Unsure of where to go, she had just started running through the streets, praying to God, "Where should I go, Lord? Help me!"

That's when she ran up to our neighbor's house and knocked on the door. When Tammy, our neighbor, opened the door, Angelica said, "Please don't call the police," and then told her what had happened.

Seeing this scared young girl on her doorstep, Tammy said, "I know a pastor and his wife down the street. They'll know what to do."

That's when they knocked on our door. We had just put our boys to bed and had settled down after a stressful week of airport drama, sickness, and seemingly endless Holy Week preparations which included hosting a Passover Seder, an interactive Good Friday service, and of course, Easter Sunday in the park that very morning.

Honestly, Wendy and I wanted nothing more in that moment than to go to bed and sleep for days. But as we listened to Angelica share her story, our hearts were desperate to help her.

Tammy turned to Angelica and said, "I know you don't know me, but I trust these people with all my heart and I know that they will take care of you, ok?"

Angelica nodded her head and quickly repeated, "Please, just don't call the police, ok?"

After Tammy left we brought Angelica inside and sat her down on the sofa. Wendy and I sat on the floor near her and just asked her to tell us her story. She was in tears a lot of the time, but eventually she got her story out.

At first, she wanted us to drive her to her Mom's house in Anaheim. "What's the phone number?" Wendy asked. But Angelica didn't know the number, she only knew the address.

I took a second to let that sink in. This teenage girl was in a stranger's house on Easter Sunday night. She had nowhere to go. No friends to call on. Even her own Mother, just a few miles away, was probably part of why she was in this girl's home in the first place. My heart broke for her.

"Angie?," I said. "I don't know your situation. But I'm guessing that your Mom's house is probably not a very safe place for you. Is it?"

She hung her head and nodded. "You're right," she said.

I asked her to consider returning to the Girl's Home, since she had affirmed that the people there were really nice and very supportive of her. But, she completely refused to go back.

"What do you want to do?" Wendy asked.

"I want to go back to Orangewood," she said. This was another children's home that she had stayed at previously.

"We can't just drive you over there and drop you off, can we?" She shook her head.

"My social worker said she can help me on Tuesday," she said.

"Ok," I said, "but by Tuesday everyone is going to know you ran away, including your social worker. By then, they won't take you to Orangewood, they'll take you back to where you ran away from, or maybe to Juvenile Hall for running away." I saw that she realized I was right.

"Can I just stay here?" she asked.

"Sure, you can stay here," Wendy said. "But the police are going to be looking for you. People are going to be worried about you, and you won't get to go back to Orangewood if you're a runaway."

We tried calling her social worker, but she didn't answer. We got a recording that said she would be back in the office on Tuesday.

So, that's when we decided to pray for wisdom. We all three held hands and bowed our heads and we asked God to honor His promise that if anyone lacks wisdom they can ask Him. So, that's exactly what we did.

We confessed that we didn't know what to do to help Angelica, but that we knew that God had a plan that was the best for her life. We prayed and then we waited.

God was faithful. He gave Wendy the answer. She looked up at me after we said "Amen" and said, "I think we should call Orangewood."

I wasn't getting it. "No one is going to answer," I said. "It's 10 p.m. on Easter Sunday evening. Who's going to be there?"

Wendy just repeated: "I think we should just call over there and see."

So, I begrudgingly looked up the phone number and dialed it, fully expecting to say, "See? I told you no one would be there," but then a live voice said, "Hello?"

So, I explained that I was trying to help a runaway girl. The woman on the phone asked me the name of the girl. "Angelica," I said. That's when the woman said, "Oh, I know Angelica! Let me talk with her."

Dumbfounded, I handed the phone over and the two of them talked for about ten minutes. Turns out the woman working the phones that night used to be Angelica's case worker.

Eventually, they made a deal: Angelica promised to go back to the girl's home for one more night and her former caseworker promised to find a way to readmit her to Orangewood. Angelica handed me back my phone. About twenty minutes later, a van pulled up in front of our house and they took Angelica back to the girl's home, safe and sound.

Now, I want you to know that if God had not told us what to do that night, Wendy and I would never have thought to call Orangewood. Before we prayed together and asked God for wisdom, neither of us had any clue about what we should do. But, once we prayed and asked God to tell us what to do, He answered us.

I could tell you a few more stories like that, but hopefully you get the point. God really does give us wisdom if we will ask Him for it. He really does speak to us by His Holy Spirit.

So, to put it in another context, even if the people who have the gift of teaching are not present for one of our church services, it's still possible for everyone else in the room to read the Scriptures, and pray, and ask God for wisdom and insight. If we do this, we should expect to receive revelation from God Himself through the Holy Spirit.

In this way, the Church is never without a teacher. The expert we require is always present because He is alive within us.

Again, this doesn't make everyone in the room a teacher, but everyone in the room does have access to hear the Teacher and to share what they learn from Him with one another.

So, it's still possible for everyone in the Body to come together under the Headship of Christ and share the gifts they've received from the Holy Spirit and participate in the life of Jesus together.

We have the living God within us. He is our instructor. Don't you think it's time we got busy listening to Him?

Excerpt from the book, *Jesus Unbound: Liberating the Word of God From the Bible*, by Keith Giles, Quoir Publishing, 2018.

7

NO MORE CIRCLES: BEYOND CERTAINTY

MARIA FRANCESCA FRENCH

After God written by Mark C. Taylor has been a seminal text for me. I was living in the South of France at the time. In a 500-year-old farmhouse on a hill in a small village in the foothills of the Alpes Maritime, more widely known for its stunning backdrop to Cary Grant in To Catch a Thief. It was January 2017. My days were free to read and write. I opened Taylor's book and read these words that have been burnt in my memory ever since, "I no longer believe in circles as I once did."[56] All of a sudden, everything I had felt,

56. Mark C. Taylor, *After God.* (Chicago: University of Chicago Press, 2007).

intuited and been silently enchanted by for years spoke audibly and articulately to me. I no longer believe that the world is made up of fixed systems and fixed meaning but dynamic measures that take us to new depths if we are prepared to see past circles. I immediately felt at home with the author's sentiments and knew that I was about to embark on the next stage of my 'deconstruction' journey. I use the term deconstruction with quotation marks because back then, even though it was only 4 years ago, that terminology wasn't as en vogue as it is today. People were, indeed, 'losing faith' or joining the ranks of a more 'progressive' or 'liberal' understanding of Christianity, but this word, *deconstruction*, as it is used now, was not available to pop culture in this way quite yet.

I was, however, smack dab in the middle of a process that had started a few years earlier for me. I didn't know what to call it, what was happening or where I might end up. There were no models to follow, not a ton of books available, or language created to address this journey I was on. It was a journey that, while painful and full of grief and loneliness, was an intuitive one. I didn't know it was happening and I didn't choose it to happen, I did, however, follow the whispers and prompts that seemed to be all around me.

N.T. Wright has used the language "whispers of a voice,"[57] describing those moments that quietly provoke you enough to disrupt your moment and have you turn around to see what is there, yet it is gone before you can apprehend it. This quick movement and slight whisper awaken you to another sort of presence there. Once you hear it, there is no unhearing it. This sort of language in my early days of seminary, which would be about 14 years ago now, started a lot for me. It inaugurated a journey that would send me flying off the circles into a spiral of meaning, asking more questions than I had answers for and quickly learning that the more I sought to learn the less I would actually know. It excited me and, more importantly, alerted me to the reality that there was more.

---

57. N.T. Wright, *Simply Christian: Why Christianity Makes Sense*. (New York: HarpersCollins, 2010).

The philosopher-theologian, John Caputo, talks about something similar using the language of haunting or, as he puts it, "hauntology."[58] Taking off from Derrida's language of "spooked," Caputo says that we are haunted by the ghosts that are to come; the ghosts of the past and the ghosts of the returned. The ghosts come to us like that of *Hamlet* or *A Christmas Carol*. Caputo says, "The spooks are trying to deconstruct Ebenezer's miserable life, which means they are trying to do him a favor."[59] In Caputo's coined "haunto-theology" he says that "we live lives of hope in the hint of the promise of what is to come" and that "we live lives of faith in the unforeseeable, in the coming of what we cannot see coming."[60]

This was very much where I was at. I had shed the pressure of trying to figure it all out and I had made peace with the haunting. The spook wakes you to that which you hadn't before seen. And once you have been spooked, the memory haunts and re-spooks and, as many of us know, we are never the same again. Caputo goes as far as to say, "that if we refuse it we fall into despair."[61] There is no going back to life as we knew it, to faith as we knew it, to God as we knew it. Life and reality are irrevocably changed and there is nothing we can do about it. To turn back would be unthinkable and unbearable despair and to suppress all that we have been prompted and provoked by. But to go forward very possibly means a fall down the rabbit hole. And that rabbit hole is an adventure; a dark, strenuous, mind bending, mind f*cking adventure. It introduces us to a new way of being which is, ultimately, a life of uncertainty and unknowing, which will eventually liberate us from constructs that we didn't know were constructs until … we did.

So, yes, four years ago reading the words of a scholar who was looking toward the future of god, after God, and listening in as he

58. John D. Caputo, *The Folly of God: A Theology of the Unconditional*, (Salem: Polebridge Press, 2016), 30.

59. Ibid, 30.

60. Ibid, 35.

61. Ibid, 34.

spoke of going around and around in circles himself, that he no longer believed in circles as he once did … in that moment, I knew I didn't either.

I grew up in New York on Long Island in an Italian American community. In my childhood I was Catholic and made all the sacraments. I went to religion class every week and, because my mother used to read me Bible stories at home, I always knew all the answers and I prided myself on that. I was bored by Catholic mass but enjoyed sitting there silently looking around at all the pomp and circumstance. I would look up and turn my head slowly to all the depths and crevasses of the elaborate sculptures, stained glass, art, gold gilded and marble depictions of biblical imagery, of domes, cross, columns and statues, all opulently speaking to a tradition in which aesthetic beauty was clearly important. While I cared not about the veneer of what was happening and what was being spoken, I could sense poignantly and mysteriously that something was happening, and I was drawn in by it. I was told the beauty I saw around me was holy and it emulated heaven. That it provided the sort of space for the spirit of God that it deserved, and one could behold a palpable and material difference between the inside and the outside; the sacred and the profane. This distinction of the sacred and profane, the holy and unholy, the outside and the inside would go on to fascinate me for years and to this day its intersections find themselves in the center of my work. I could sense there was a delineation where there should not be, even at such a young age. That these categories were, at best, a feeble and futile attempt at understanding what seems isn't available to understanding.

I remember when I was around 10-years old, making my first confession to a Priest in my parish. I was in with the priest for over 30 minutes and everyone wondered what was happening. Most children had gone in for a minute or two, confessed a bad word they said at school or giving a dirty look to someone. I didn't really understand this idea of confession and thinking hard about all I had done wrong and then telling it to someone. So, I just decided to talk. I talked about my life and what I was going through and if there was something off, something to possibly ask forgiveness for, then it was simply a matter of circumstance. Even then I knew everything had a context and that it was all connected. Nothing was disassociated from who we are and what our lives consisted of. And why should we be punished for it? Nothing existed in a vacuum, not least of which religion and how we understand god. But I didn't know that yet. I didn't know it for a very long time. But I must have already been spooked by it at such a young and tender age. Because I had a very deep sense that there was something around bigger and better than me. It caused me to be silent and it caused me to look up. I was a little afraid but also excited. Whatever it was I was sensing I knew it was for me. Which is why I followed the course of a metaphysical, supernatural, and interventionist God.

A few years later my mother moved my sister and I on from the Catholic church to the biggest Evangelical-Charismatic church on Long Island. This is where I spent my adolescence and teen years deeply involved in all of the things (if you know you know). It provided really well what most churches like this provide really well: community. For years, I built friendships that would carry me through a very tumultuous time in my life and provide a sense of belonging, safety, and love. For the most part, big Evangelical youth group settings do an OK job at this. I was surrounded by people who wanted to pour into my life and be there for me. I had lots of opportunities to go away to camps and retreats where I would have the time of my life during the day and also worship and learn my heart out in the evenings. I was the girl who sat in the first chair in the first row. All. The. Time. Proximity was still important. A hold over from my Catholic days, I'm sure. But whatever was happening I loved it. Hands up in the air, ecstatically engaging with God, feeling the fullness of what I believed to be the presence of Jesus and just feeling so loved. I did all the mission trips because I couldn't just take, I had to give too, right? And, of course, signed my virginity over to God by signing a card as part of a *True Love Waits* campaign that my youth group launched. I petitioned my public school board to have a bible club after school each week. When the talent shows and concerts came around I always sang the Christians songs and I did it all for Jesus. I imagined him sitting in the front row, in his shepherd garb , as depicted in those white European paintings in your church, and knowing he was proud of me . Yep. I did all the things.

I talk about a time in my life that was over 20 years ago now, but I can still remember with such clarity. I wish some of it were different. I can see years later how some of it harmed me, but I'm also very much owning and in possession of my own journey and my own story.

When I was eighteen, I moved to Minneapolis, MN and attended a Bible College. I was full swing Pentecostal and spent those four years doing all the things you would imagine an on fire, born again, Charismatic, Evangelical young Christian to be doing. The ministry leadership, the prayer meetings, the worship nights, the prophesying, the volunteering, the mission trips, the street ministry and an all-out just saving everyone for Jesus.

But even though I was fully involved in my Pentecostal faith, things were changing. When I moved on to seminary, I started to shed the Pentecostal bit of my faith. As I found myself in a more academic setting I found less need for this charismatic expression of my faith. This started the first bit of push back that I would receive from family and friends for many years to come. This was my first taste of anti-intellectualism in Evangelicalism and conservative Christianity. I didn't know what to call it. But I knew it hurt. It invalidated my experience and let me know that I had moved from the fold of what was acceptable and what was not. Although, I didn't have the language to articulate a response at the time.

It would take me many years to gather up and create the language that I needed to talk about this process that was, ultimately, a demythologizing, disentangling, disentwining and a deconverting experience. Life is a spiral, not a circle. Why would you want to keep going around and around within the same fixed system and continuing to traverse the same terrain? Never knowing anything new, never experiencing the fullness of your humanity and life and never risking it all for the promise of all that might be coming?

The current conversation on deconstruction is an interesting one. It is one I have sat back and taken some time to listen to closely.

When it first started a few years ago (maybe a little less), I was more interested in the language used to describe the process, than the process itself. Firstly, I don't think that for most people the kind of deconstruction they are referring to is philosophical deconstruction as understood via Jacques Derrida and I was wondering how the term got connected to this pop culture process of leaving church. I also thought that perhaps there is a better word. This thought was purely based on my own experience which I wouldn't so much classify as deconstructing but perhaps more of a *devaluing*, or refiguring, of certain things within my Christianity. As I put less value on one thing, I put more value on another. Devolving was another term that came to mind, as one set of values was devolving another was evolving.

Within the deconstruction conversation today there seems to be an exchange going on. The exchange of one set of ideas for another, a deconstructing in order to reconstruct with ideas that we like better. It's a lifting of the curtain to see the man behind it and to expose and topple the whole thing for the house of cards that it seems to be. It has all become a war of words when it comes to certainty, objectivity, empirical realities and facticity. Talk about circles … these sorts of conversation will keep us going around and around with very little transformative outcomes in the end and we must be on guard for going down paths that lead to nowhere.

For example, Evangelical understanding of inerrancy and infallibility of Scripture simply cannot hold up given what we know of the Biblical texts, how they were formed, canonized, and handed down. So, we say that Scripture isn't authoritative because it clearly isn't inerrant or infallible. It is full of mistakes, historical slip-ups, empirical no shows, and lacks the facticity words like inerrancy and infallibly claim. So there. We have debunked the Bible, right? But here's the thing. What if we took those categories off the table? Because they aren't proper categories to talk about anything literary, storied, or sacred for that matter.

If Scripture is freed from the confines of inerrancy by traditional theists and liberated from the drudge of the 'gotcha' moment by Atheists, then maybe we can have a conversation about Scripture that it actually deserves. The kind of conversation that takes into account its narrative, its human authors, the cultures and contexts in which it was written, the themes we find throughout, the accurate pictures painted to us to communicate theological truths about how god has been manifested in particular times and places throughout the history of a particular people, and what this story might be saying to us today. A theological understanding of Scripture that releases the need to be empirically true or not true. I think we can talk about authority in a way that gives it a bit more movement and a bit more plasticity. That is the conversation I'm interested it.

I think this is what happens when we exchange belief for faith. Belief tells us that we have to choose a side, that we have to choose a category and presents us with acceptable options that fall somewhere on the theist/atheist spectrum. Belief, as we understand it today, forces us to answer questions like, 'Do you think Jesus literally rose from the dead?' or 'Do you believe in a literal Adam and Eve or a literal flood?' Belief backs us into a corner to make decisions on the objective existence of a metaphysical god or not. Or, perhaps, if we are working on that theist/atheist spectrum, the middle of that continuum might present a more acceptable god. One that is less angry, less wrathful, in less need of penal atonement, and one that is more inclusive, loving, and inviting with a main aim of justice. The thing about that new, nicer and more acceptable god is that we are still buying and selling in currencies of existence and trading in certainty. We still find we are affirming some sort of objective existence of god, perhaps an interventionist one perhaps not. And if one finds themself on the atheist side of the spectrum then we are still trading in currencies of certainty by affirming god does not exist, objectively and empirically.

I am not interested in this conversation. It doesn't get us any-where. And I think it leaves a lot of brokenness in its wake. Part of, what I think, is a healthy deconstruction process is to first and foremost understand that you are about to answer an invitation from a ghost, from a whisper-one that beckons you toward a real-ity of uncertainties. If we are to dismantle or deconstruct anything it must be our addiction to certainty first. Once we do that, we are free to blow past categories of existence, objectivity, metaphysicality, supernaturalism, categories like literal vs non-literal and inerrant vs errant, because they simply don't matter anymore. Philosophies that need to account for god and religion in the non-literal sense become superfluous and irrelevant and our faith becomes free to pursue god, life, and our humanity outside of classifications of certainty and assuredness. Gianni Vattimo in his book, *After Christianity*, talks about how when god no longer is synonymous with metaphysicality we can believe again. When we become aware that "the vision of being as … objectivist metaphysics is untenable, we are left with the biblical notion of creation."[62]

My seminary days led me to a faith stage that was post-Charismatic and post-Evangelical. After a while, the sky simply could no longer hold. Meaning the big God in the sky ran out of steam and I had come to the end of it and the end of myself. But it wasn't the end of my Christianity. It was truly the beginning of what was next. Years later I found myself post-theist and post-Christian. And it wasn't because I had made a distinct choice to deconstruct or even move in a different direction. I didn't feel hostile or angry. It was simply that things that used to make sense no longer did. But it also didn't make sense to simply check my entire religious identity as a Christian at the door and just be done with it. I knew there were ways of engaging my faith narrative past an understanding of a supernatural god, past constructs of after life, sexual purity, concepts of original sin and the number one Christian requirement of having a personal relationship with the person of Jesus. I just didn't know what those ways were yet.

At 31 I found myself newly divorced (which is a whole other part of my story for another time) and living on my own. But I still found myself nominally connected to and interested in Christianity. I'm not sure how, but I did. I didn't pray or read my bible for devotional reasons. I didn't go to church and, outside of my vocation as

62. Gianni Vattimo, trans by Luca D'Isanto, *After Christianity*. (New York: Columbia University Press, 2002), 6.

administration at a seminary, I didn't have a spiritual community that I was involved with. I felt alone and I was starting my life over completely.

Over the next year and a half or so I sort of coasted, theologically. I was working hard at my seminary job, helping to get a new school of theology off the ground and traveling a ton. God seemed silent. Which was fine. I was silent, too. I preferred this to the many years of how vocal we had both been. I was ready for a deep and long rest. I wasn't in a hurry and I had no destination in mind. It was painful and a bit lonely, but it was peaceful.

Between the divorce, not going to church and my slow and silent turn of faith, a lot of family and friends thought I had just lost it. And by that, I mean had lost my faith and taken an atheistic turn. Looking back, it's hard to recall exactly what that time in my life was all about but I know it wasn't atheistic. It wasn't even agnostic. It was just a time for me *to be*. I was sitting in sack cloth and ashes and watching the last bit of the embers of my God (my understanding of God) die out. And I was totally fine with it. I never said goodbye, I never said thanks for everything. I never had a final prayer or moment. It was a natural movement away from something that seemed to vaporize over time. There was nothing there to say goodbye to and I very acutely and distinctly felt that. I was confident in my choice, even though I didn't know what was next.

Soon after that time I found myself off to live in the South of France for what would be 6 months which turned into a year and a half. It was an incredible time in my life. So much travel and beauty and adventure. So many amazing people and culture and play and rest. A lot of rosé, sun and sea. It was during this time I took it upon myself to study for the first time in a long time; to really study this new area that some were calling post theism, as well as Radical Theology. I knew I was no longer a theist, but I certainly wasn't an atheist. I was post theist. I was post the big other, the divine care giver that lives in our hearts. I had moved through it and I was done with it and was moving on from it. It was behind me now but very much still in my memory. I never sought to deny the reality of that experience in my life or what it meant to me and also what it produced in my life. But I wasn't there any longer and I never would be ever again. And that was totally ok, and I was at peace with it.

Sitting in that farmhouse in the South of France, there was another book I read as closely as Taylor's and that was *Anatheism* by Richard Kearney. Anatheism is the idea of returning to God after God and returning to faith after faith. The ana in Anatheism being the idea of *back again*, *anew* and *to return*. Kearney talks about how things like belief, existence and absolute realities have to be of the table. And I agree because there simply isn't enough imagination to be had there. There is no room for it. And imagination is what we need for the future of faith, or for our faith to have future. Kearney defines the anathesist moment as "The 'holy insecurity' of radical openness to the strange."[63] He says that this moment is "available to anyone who experiences instants of deep disorientation, doubt, or dread, when we are no longer sure exactly who we are or where we are going."[64] He goes on to say that these sorts of moments "may visit us in the middle of the night"[65] even. Like a ghost, a haunting if you will. Something that will whisper to us and cause mayhem that cannot be undone and it catches us up in a spin of disorientation that delivers us to another way of thinking and to another way of seeing. A realm that deals not in absolutes, but with the knowledge that if there is an absolute to be found that is requires our subjectivity as a means to chip away at seeing any possible objectivity there may be. Kearney says that "the absolute requires pluralism to avoid absolutism."[66] Our plurality of thought allows us to return

63. Richard Kearney, *Anatheism: Returning to God After God*, (New York: Columbia University Press, 2010), 5.

64. Ibid, 5.

65. Ibid, 5.

66. Ibid, xiv.

to 'god' again and again, each time being informed by our spiraling journeying provoked by ghosts, spooks, and, of course, specter.[67]

As I started to learn that engaging faith was about being at home in uncertainty, embracing the lack and letting go of the tyranny of religion that promises to make us whole, the more I found myself living with less existential angst, less fear of death and an openness to life and what was to come, than ever before.

And there it was-Taylor's sentiments on circles. The culmination of all I had gone through. Of all I had lived through and lived to tell. "I no longer believe in circles as I once did." I was never looking to offload my Christianity. I was only ever looking to continue on this path of faith I had been on my whole life. Even now I look back and see a seamless journey. Everything has been built on what has come before it. Things have had to be healed and patched up, sometimes reworked and reconfigured, but the journey deeper into life has always been there-it is just ever changing.

John Caputo in his book, *The Folly of God*, says, "Generally, when something is deconstructed, we should greet it as "good news" and be grateful, even if sometimes it leaves us standing on our beds in the middle of the night all atremble."[68] That is the thing about being haunted. The specter disrupts and interrupts that status quo of our Christianity and our human experience and it shakes us to our very core because, usually, our entire identity has been built on our belief systems and the relationship we have formed with our god(s). And when it is disrupted, it has potential to ensue quiet the crisis. But somehow it is always good news in the end for the one being spooked. It certainly was good news for me.

People used to ask me often what I believed. It was an uncomfortable question to be asked. The discomfort with this word and concept of belief had been years in the making. I couldn't articulate then like I can now, and I would get reluctantly and relentlessly

67. John Caputo often uses the term specter to describe the weak god; the one who insists. See *The Weakness of God* (2006) and *The Insistence of God* (2013) for further reading.

68. Caputo, *The Folly of God*, 30.

sucked into conversations and answering questions that I had no interest in answering. Looking back, it was a bit abusive and a bit berating how friends and family refused to let me be. But it is clear to me now that my freedom of choice and my personal autonomy made them uncomfortable, and they didn't know what to do with it because it didn't fit their (narrow) narrative of Christianity. And I get it because I was there once. I don't answer those questions anymore. My faith, and my engagement with it, isn't based on what I believe and what I don't believe. My belief does nothing for the thing I say I believe in and vice versa. Rather than focus on the belief in or of something, I much more prefer to soak deep down into the theological journey faith might take us on if we can liberate ourselves from the entanglement of belief. Belief harasses and maligns faith. They are not the same and often belief is the enemy of faith. It keeps is static and immovable. It keeps it in a circle with no plausible or possible way to go. When we remove belief, the same way when we bypass existence and being, we can open up the categories for faith, god, religion and meaning in ways that are endless and boundless.

The deconstruction conversation happening at the moment is all about change. It's changing away from a context and a construct that no longer works for us and/or has potentially harmed and, in some cases, abused us. Every generation of Christians has their way of saying WTF. However, a main game changer in the deconstruction conversation is digitality and social media platforms. The conversations are growing and becoming more networked than they ever could have without digital means. It is truly a wonderful thing for people to have this kind of space to work out their issues with belief, religion and some of the harm Christianity has caused many. Anyone who says deconstructing needs to happen a certain way or within a certain type of community is wrong. The conversation you have with your faith is all your own. And it will look completely different from one person to the next. We will find community in our shared experiences of it all, yes. But it is a deeply personal experience that is unique to our own journeys. It is something to feel

122   BEFORE YOU LOSE YOUR MIND

good about and be proud of because you have moved through and survived something quite profound.

There is meaning beyond metaphysicality, there is Jesus beyond saviorism, there is life beyond certainty, and faith beyond belief. Spooked by ghosts returning from the past and coming at us from the future, whispering no more circles, it is untenable to stay the same. When we deconstruct, we don't do it along a continuum, we do it deep and down into the abyss, where certainty is condemned as myth and fairytale, mystery is a tenet to live by and we measure our meaning making mechanisms, like god and religion, by their ability to be life affirming. The risk is great, but if paradigms can be shifted and expectations subverted and turned upside, you will find yourself hopping the track of the circle and living more deeply and integrally human than you ever thought possible because the impossible[69] is now what we are after.

Written exclusively for this book by Maria Francesca French, 2021.

---

69. John Caputo often uses language like impossible up against the possible.

8

THE WAY TO SALVATION

JOSH ROGGIE

I live in Colorado Springs, Colorado. It is one of my favorite places that I have ever been. I am thankful to live here. There is so much beauty with Pikes Peak visible from almost anywhere in the city. There are some great local restaurants. Most of my book was written in about 6 different amazing coffee shops. The weather is just awesome with a nice, warm summer and no humidity. The winters can get a little chilly, but it pales in comparison to my childhood years in upstate New York.

There is one thing, though. I see a lot of homeless and impoverished people. There are quite a few panhandlers downtown and along a lot of the busier intersections. I am sure you have noticed this wherever you live, too. They hold signs saying "anything helps" or "retired vet needs help." By the way, it floors me that the U.S.

government will pour \$693,058,000,000[70] into our military in 2019 and yet there are so many homeless veterans unable to get the help they need to overcome their physical and mental debilitating injuries.

Whether vets or not, these homeless people are usually really dirty and unkempt and must be so dehydrated being in the hot sun for hours at a time. What a tragedy that we consider people like that to be an inconvenience. It should be really uncomfortable to see homeless people, but it can't end there with that feeling. It doesn't seem like Jesus would respond that way.

The state of Colorado has approximately 10,857 homeless people as of January 2018.[71] That is nearly 2% of the nation's homeless population. Colorado also happens to have an overall population of nearly 2% of the nation's overall population. So it would seem we are about average in regards to how many homeless people live in Colorado. Colorado Springs itself has 1,562 homeless[72] in a city of approximately 472,688.[73] That's a lower percentage, but it is still a sad day when there are so many suffering in our city and our state.

One more statistic for you. Colorado Springs has over 420 churches citywide.[74] And no, that is not a pot joke. That's not even counting other faiths such as Jewish, Muslim, etc. There are also dozens of Christian-based non profit organizations such as Focus on the Family, Compassion International, Young Life, etc. that are based out of the city. Colorado Springs is essentially the Mecca of conservative Christianity. But that's a shitty thing to be known

70. https://comptroller.defense.gov/Portals/45/Documents/defbudget/fy2020/FY20_Green_Book.pdf

71. https://www.usich.gov/homelessness-statistics/co/

72. https://www.csindy.com/TheWire/archives/2019/05/21/point-in-time-count-shows-homeless-population-leveling-out-in-colorado-springs

73. The overall population is the estimate as of July 2018 found at https://www.census.gov/quickfacts/coloradospringscitycolorado.

74. http://www.world-guides.com/north-america/usa/colorado/colorado-springs/colorado_springs_churches.html

for. It misses the point. If each church in the city just adopted four homeless people, the homeless epidemic would essentially be solved overnight. But that has not happened and those homeless people continue to suffer. A great prophet once said that we will be known by how we love each other.

Why do we allocate so much time and money to winning a culture war focused on making stores say "Merry Christmas" instead of "Happy Holidays" while a homeless person is freezing to death right outside the doors of our cozy churches? Why do we worry about what laws are on the ballot when there are women who can't afford to be pregnant because their already born kids can't get enough to eat even as we throw away several pounds of uneaten food at our church potlucks? So many times, Jesus did a miracle for a broken body before ever bringing up a single word of repentance. Sounds like a strategy the church should consider next time they are holding anti-abortion signs or picketing against homosexuals or whoever else they decide to bully on any given day.

The good news is that there are people helping. These are people who care and want to make a difference. We have organizations in Colorado Springs, such as Springs Rescue Mission, that are dedicated to ending homelessness by providing a warm place to stay and a recovery program to re-integrate into society. Which brings up the real question for me. Do I personally care? I have the luxury of being frustrated at not having enough time to write, because my regular 9–5 job can be mentally taxing. All while I sit on my comfortable couch in my warm living room playing video games.

I make very little effort to directly help. I might occasionally donate a couple bucks or a turkey during Thanksgiving. But that doesn't really cost me anything. Sure, it is a few dollars, but it doesn't involve me doing something I am uncomfortable with that would leave a lasting mark.

Instead, I complain about the ways in which I am dissatisfied with not creating enough or doing things that I would deem more meaningful. Interesting that I want something more meaningful and yet make so little effort toward meaningfully helping the less fortunate.

So what the hell am I doing with my life? I think I am learning, maybe even as I type this right now. I am trying to do everything I want without trusting God. I say I trust Him and I truly do want to be trusting of Him, but my lifestyle shows that I have done as much as possible to remove my need of God from my life. There was a time when I had trusted God very deeply. Probably not on a biblical level the way that Mother Theresa did, but I was taking baby steps in the right direction. When my wife, Dannika, and I decided to move back to Colorado from Missouri, we had put a down payment and signed a lease on an apartment before we even got there.

Neither of us had completed a Bachelor's degree at the time. There was not a job between us. We had less than 3 months worth of savings put together to get us by until we found work. We did have the luxury of both sets of our parents living in the city we were moving to, and they absolutely helped through that process, but otherwise we were very much making a leap of faith.

I look back and question what the hell I was thinking. I needed a job fast. I had a couple interviews lined up for the first week I was there, but these were not surefire jobs by any means. One was at a bank that clearly focused on sales (something I had almost no experience in) and another was at a call center doing cell phone tech support (something I had no experience in—it was 2013 and I didn't even own a smartphone yet). To top it off, I was hoping against hope that I would get a job that paid well enough that my wife wouldn't have to find work unless she wanted to. There were a lot of reasons we wanted to do that, but it was largely so she could pursue the things that she cared about at home. We also needed health insurance to come from somewhere.

It seemed like such a long shot that I would not only get a job, but one that would fulfill all of our desires *and* happen in the necessary time frame. Unbelievably, I landed the call center position in my first week of job hunting. And it did fulfill all of our needs at that time. My wife has worked at different points since then, but she has been able to choose the jobs she wants and focus on writing and all of her other interests.

It seemed like God gave us everything we had asked for. However, contentment has still been difficult to find. Apparently, I should have asked God for even more.

There's another way Dannika and I have been trying to trust God. Traditionally, the amount of your money you are told to give to the church is 10%, which is a tithe. Tithe and 10% are considered to be synonymous among most Christians, though I think that kinda misses the point.

I would say that the number isn't super important, but 10% a solid starting point if you're wanting to know what to do. The real point is not in percentages, but in how giving and free you are with your money. The bigger sacrifice it is for you, the greater blessing it is. That's true beyond money, as well. The way you give of your time is also indicative of your heart and your love for people. But the Church seems more preoccupied with your money.

As I said, 10% is a good starting point for some people. My wife and I thought so when we first got married. And we had this idea in our head. What if we increased that number by a percent for each year we are married? After one year of marriage, we would increase our giving to 11%. After five years of marriage, we would be at 15% giving. After 15 years, we will be at 25% giving. So on and so forth.

And that's exactly what we have done. We want to increase our faith and reliance on God more each year. And a funny thing has happened through this.

1. We always have enough. We don't necessarily have a lot. There are certainly others better off than us. But we pay our bills and we have the pleasure of eating out sometimes or occasionally going to a concert or movie.

2. I am still always *so* stressed about money!

How is it possible that I could find a way to tangibly show God I want to trust him more, but still find myself more stressed because of those same steps I am doing trying to convey how I trust him! It's a paradox. I wish I could sit here and write that increasing our giving removed all of my anxieties and even enabled us to establish a new soup kitchen and adopt 15 orphan children. That's just not true, though.

Instead, I became more preoccupied with scarcity and my sin was to worry about my financial future. This just may be the most common sin among the middle and upper class in America today. One of the wealthiest people groups at any point in history and we are quite literally worried to death about money.

Anxiety and worry are certainly my own personal thorns in the side. So maybe the problem isn't my job or my massive school debt or the way I spend my money. Maybe the problem is that I think about these things way more than I think about that homeless woman on the corner who would probably be content if I stopped and just talked with her.

What if I just asked her what her name was and how she ended up here? What if I asked him to tell me what he really needs instead of tossing some pocket change at the problem? What if I looked you in the eyes and asked who you really are beyond your shame? What if that is the way to my own salvation?

In truth, I don't feel much shame over these perspectives any longer. I have found that the more I have been able to release the shame of my story, the more I have found freedom in the blindspots that I have yet to discover. The less pressure I place on myself to be perfect, the more I realize God is willing and able to accept me as imperfect.

My lack of faith is a poor perspective on who I am and what I am called to be. But God doesn't hate me or see me as a failure for struggling with trust. Other Christians don't seem to hate me, either. I don't get private messages from people telling me that they are worried for my soul and praying for my salvation. Maybe there will be an uptick of this as more people read my book. But even if that does happen, I will know that those messages would be a reflection of how they view their own mishaps more so than it would impact my value.

Because it seems like the person who judges me the most is me. I feel shame over my self-perception. I am my own harshest critic. Of course I am hopeful that people read my story and get something out of it, but at this point I am finding that the hardest part is just finishing it and getting it in front of people to read. It seems much easier to give up.

I keep telling myself nobody is going to read my book anyway. It is going to ruffle more feathers than it is worth since nobody is going to like it. I will lose respect from people that I have been trying for years to convince I am a writer once they see what my writing is actually like.

For so long, my lifestyle has been one of limiting possible hurt. I rarely ever asked girls out when I was in high school, because I feared rejection. I still play my finances as conservatively as possible and don't ever go for broke—even if it could make all my dreams come true. I don't write enough, work out enough, help others enough, put myself out there and let myself be known enough. I am quiet when I should speak. I say a dumb joke instead of my meaningful thoughts when I do actually say something.

When I was an early twenty something, I had a very handy self-help trick to functionally do the risky things that I knew I should do. I would be on the verge of asking for the girl's number or applying for a job or buying plane tickets to travel. I would feel that pit in my stomach that made me question if this is something I really should do. I would try to analyze every detail and finally clear my mind and just say, "Screw it!"

It only works if you literally say the words out loud. And then I would pop the question, buy the tickets, etc.

I guess that is where I'm at now. I am saying "Screw it!" and putting myself out there. I'm still a mess in my lifestyle, but I am moving towards my salvation and freedom. I've got plenty more shame to share, but in my shameful state it is nice to have a brief reprieve and consider the shame that I am escaping with every word I type.

I have changed as a person over the last several years in ways that challenge my own words. The clearest example is in regards to this chapter and the practice my wife and I did with our tithing and the increased giving each year.

We don't do that anymore. At one point, we stopped giving the increased amount and went back to the standard 10%. There were several reasons for it, the biggest being that it became an obligation that I couldn't do with a giving heart any longer. I also felt hamstrung financially in pursuing other things that I felt God was putting on my heart, things that those extra funds could help with.

And several months of going back to the standard level, Dannika and I decided that the church we were attending was no longer the right place for us to be. I don't have much to share on that front, because it is still so fresh and "last-minute" through the writing process. All that to say, we no longer have a church to give our tithe to and we are very much revamping our whole perspective on what is right and holy in regards to money management.

Some people would probably try to cast shame on us for this, seeing this change as a loss of faith. We feel no shame over it whatsoever. I only include it in this story for the sake of transparency. We still seek new ways to sacrifice more of ourselves and to give more to others. The theme of this chapter remains unchanged. The way to salvation is not in rituals, even the most beautiful ones. The way to transcendence is in meeting people exactly where they are, especially those most hurt and forgotten. This is a lesson I had learned from spending time with hurt people, but little did I know that my family would be the hurting people in need of help.

Adapted from the book, *Shame: An Unconventional Memoir*, by Josh Roggie, Quoir Publishing, 2020.

9

OPEN HANDS

BRANDON DRAGAN

Don't deconstruct.

There. I said it.

Don't do it.

Or, if you do, only deconstruct to the extent that you reach pre-determined answers.

Our answers.

Remember, we're supposed to hold fast to the profession of our faith.

If you start doubting one area, what's to say you won't doubt the rest?

After all, there can only be one truth.

And you should consider yourself lucky—blessed, I should say—that out of the thousands of different religions on the planet, and the tens of thousands of Christian denominations alone, you stumbled upon the right one.

Oh, and make sure you put your love gift in the basket as it goes by … you know, above and beyond your weekly tithe, because the parsonage needs a new jacuzzi tub in the master.

CREED

It would almost be comical if it wasn't so harmful, right? If people weren't actually being abused at the hands of a system designed to keep us all in line.

But first, let me get this out in the open: I'm still a confessing Christian.

I affirm the Apostles' Creed. And I don't do it because I'm convinced of its truth in an intellectual way. I affirm it because I chose to. It connects me with a beautiful faith tradition and I like that.

I affirm the Apostles' Creed because I hold it in open hands, rather than clenched fists.

I first came across that concept in a truly astounding little book called Bring Prayer into Your Life With Open Hands by Henri Nouwen, and it's become something of a Rosetta Stone by which I view the world.

So I say that I hold it in open hands because I might be wrong.

And I'm fine with that.

TURTLES & TABERNACLES

Another step backward, so you'll know a little about where I'm coming from.

I was raised in northeastern New Jersey—not exactly a hotbed of church culture, but I came from a family where faith was important.

You see, my grandparents on my mom's side were born in the Soviet Union and only escaped after being displaced by the Second World War. They came to the states with the knowledge that their

Christian brothers and sisters left behind were suffering unimaginable evils because of their faith.

So being born in America, where you could practice your faith freely and openly, was a privilege not to be taken lightly. Taking a serious faith seriously was a responsibility you owed to those believers huddled in secret meetings, those brave brothers and sisters clinging to their faith in a Gulag, and those martyrs who had already lost their lives for the sake of Jesus.

I'd say that's pretty heavy for a five year old, but I was all about it.

In fact, I remember praying within earshot of an adult relative one day—I want to say I was still in kindergarten—and thanking God that he *"could even love scum like me."*

The only reason I remember this particular prayer is that after I was done, this person said, "Maybe if you pray in front of people—like in Sunday school or something—don't say 'scum.' Say 'sinner' instead."

Think about that.

The level of indoctrination.

And I don't just mean me … I mean, check out the level that my relatives had been force-fed the Kool-aid.

He was not correcting my theology—the belief that I, the Ninja Turtle obsessed, sensitive kid with the sandy blonde baby curls, was *scum in God's eyes.*

What he was correcting, was *how to display that faith for the approval of others.*

And man, what a damaging, soul-smothering message that was.

(Caveat here: my family is amazing. We have all been on our own journeys but have still journeyed together.)

But at that point in my life, I literally believed that you could "lose your salvation" at the drop of a hat. Much groveling was required to stay in God's good graces.

And ongoing groveling, too.

As in, if I died in my sleep, having *one sin* that remained unconfessed, I would spend eternity burning in a hell-fire that no stop, drop, and roll the fireman at school taught us could save me from.

And this all stemmed from this idea that God is so holy and human beings are so inherently flawed and evil, that we should be thrilled with anything better than eternity in hell … Including a life of self-immolation and salvation anxiety.

Speaking of kindergarten (and those blessed, pizza-eating mutants), I brought a Ninja Turtles crayon box in to my conservative Christian private school. Maybe the second day of school, my teacher went on a rant about neither she—nor the stern, oft-red-faced and yelling principal—liked the Ninja Turtles, because *God didn't like stories about mutants or ninjas.*

I spent the entire school year with that box face down on my desk so that she would not catch a glimpse of the evil, half-shelled objects of God's wrath.

And the thing is, I wasn't really worried about getting in "trouble" about it …

I was worried that she would think less of me.

My next early church memory was listening to a very, very special guest who came to speak in my third grade Sunday school class.

This guest was to be revered, honored, and even imitated.

This person was *a missionary.*

And not any old missionary.

This person was a missionary *in Africa.*

And this missionary told us about how awful things were in Africa—starvation and disease and backwards tribal bush people who worship the devil and are possessed by demons—and how the only hope for these poor, sorry Africans was Jesus.

(Side note: *racist much!?*)

That's why this missionary needed our money—*they literally asked eight year olds for money*—so that this missionary could tell more Africans about Jesus.

I remember another kid raising his hand and asking why we didn't just feed the starving children, since they were … you know … starving.

And because, you know, that *actually seemed to be the problem …*

This missionary's answer was burned into my mind and was perhaps the earliest step in my deconstruction: *"Well, we don't have enough to feed everyone, but we can tell everyone about Jesus, and that way, they can at least go to heaven."*

Ten year old me thought: something doesn't sound right about that.

Thirty-six year old me will reinterpret for you: *that's some steaming horse shit right there.*

A couple years later, I was struck by the thought that other people had other religions, and that those others religions taught that if I didn't believe in that religion, I would end up in hell.

So I asked my grandfather one day: "Papa, how do we know that the God we believe in is the right God?"

His response?

"That's the devil in your mind. Don't ask that question or he'll will get a foothold."

Hold that faith with closed fists, young'un.

I remember even then being massively dissatisfied with that answer, but I tried to take it in stride.

(Another side note: my grandfather was, is, and always will be one of my absolute heroes. He will always remain one of the best people, and yes, one of the truest, most merciful Christians, I've ever known.)

Then in high school, my family had a major falling out with the only church I'd ever called home, and things got weird.

I started having all sorts of doubts that my clenched knuckles strained against. I specifically remember waking up one morning and thinking—I believe in spiritual warfare? Angels and demons and all sorts of spirits flying around my head that I cannot see or detect, other than maybe some vague creepy feeling if I'm lucky? Sounds like a fairy tale.

But of course, you have to *hold on* to your faith. So I did my best.

For a period of time, my family ended up driving to Brooklyn every Sunday morning (and many Tuesday nights) to attend a massive, Pentecostal, speak-in-tongues kind of church. Let me say here that this was not what we were used to, but there was something undeniably alive and healing in that place, and we needed that.

It was in that tabernacle that I opened myself up to the idea that God really does move among us and through us. I started "feeling" God all over the place, and that became almost like a drug.

And this place had like, advertised miracles happening. As in, they put out DVDs about people in their church who had been instantaneously and miraculously healed from disease, abuse, and decades of drug addiction.

The funny thing was … that kind of thing never seemed to happen around *me*.

I was taught, just *pray more* if you want to see God work like that.

So I did.

Still nothing? *Read the Bible more.*

So I did.

Still nothing? *Worship more.*

And I did.

Still nothing.

The relationships around me were still broken.

Friends were were still battling addiction.

And I was still convinced that I was scum in God's eyes, because otherwise, he would show up …

Wouldn't he?

My knuckles were turning red.

Just hold on, Brandon. Hold on to it.

Then, I was introduced to C.S. Lewis my senior year at the super-conservative Christian high school I attended. And that allowed me to breathe and relax my grip a little. See, I learned from C.S. Lewis that you didn't have to sacrifice your intellectual integrity to have belief in God. That's a great lesson.

What followed, however … not so much.

You see, that led me down the rabbit hole of apologetics.

I read books about how God could be proved to exist, and how if I still had doubts, I should remember the book of Job: *who was I to question God?*

(Remember, I was still scum!)

I was taught to be ready to give an answer that would defend the faith (my Christian high school's "mascot" was a "Defender"—a cartoon dressed up in Roman garb who was supposed to spur us on to victory not only on the basketball court, but in the courts of our hearts. Or something like that … didn't make much sense then either …).

Again—closed fists.

I even started reading books by prominent atheists simply in order to criticize their arguments in the margins with all the knowledge I'd amassed about how wrong they were.

I thought I'd arrived.

I understood it all.

It all made sense.

Until it didn't.

CRACKS

From there, it was off to Nashville to pursue my dream of being a singer-songwriter in the mold of John Mayer because after all, it was 2003. I pursued that dream for a while, and might have actually been mediocre, but then life swooped in. I married my college sweetheart and started working real jobs. I wanted a stable life, kids, cats, and I don't know, something more. I still thought about maybe being a worship leader, or even "planting" my own church, but that was also a lot of work.

My wife and I tried church after church in and around Nashville, and just didn't feel like we belonged anywhere.

In one place, the pastor mocked the recently released movie, The DaVinci Code, devoting an entire forty minute message to repeating things like, "How dare they question the Wurrrd of Gaaaawd!" These proclamations were met with thunderous applause, by the way.

In another place, the preacher devoted an entire message to mocking fat people. I'm literally not kidding. He tried using the part of the Bible where it says Samuel was impressed by David's appearance (gay Freudian slip anyone?) to tell us that it was a sin not to be lean and muscled.

On yet another stop, a man who knew we were visiting approached me during the alter call and told me he had a word from God specifically for me. I was so excited—so ready for God to finally show up and speak into my life in a supernatural way. The man put his hand on my head and made several very bold statements about my life—you're a student athlete, you attend such and such university, etc.—*all of which were wrong.*

Which led me wonder ... are we just making all of this up as we go?

Then I started reading Rob Bell.

You probably haven't heard of him.

(That's sarcasm).

And I remember thinking, "Eww, this is uncomfortable ... If we start doubting *these* beliefs, where do we stop? We can't just doubt *all of them* ... right?"

Then the thought struck me: *why not?*

I mean, if it's true, it'll withstand honest doubt ... right?

My grip loosened ever so slightly.

ONE LAST SQUEEZE

Then, I decided to jump in deep one last time—to let God prove himself to me once and for all. I took a job in ministry with a very conservative organization doing fantastic work and making a difference in the lives of very vulnerable people.

I thought this was it—I thought God had taken me on this long road to lead me to this particular place where I would finally find my niche, finally see my miracles, and finally experience fullness, peace, and a life of faith that would come as second nature.

Only, I had to raise my own support (meaning, my own salary).

That's okay! I'm was going to jump in!

I was prayed over and counseled by more spiritual mentors than I can remember that I would never be in God's debt—*he would always show up* just when I needed him the most.

When our mortgage was due and we lacked seven hundred thirty six dollars and twenty nine cents to make the payment, I could expect a check to miraculously show up in the mail for seven hundred thirty six dollars and twenty nine cents!

This was going to be amazing!

Well, six months and twelve thousands dollars of credit card and medical debt later, it certainly seemed that the post was running awfully slow.

And when I brought this up to those same people who had told me to trust the promises of God, suddenly, the situation seemed to be conspicuously *my fault*.

How is your prayer life?

Did you pray over those particular support letters individually?

Do you have unconfessed sin issues?

So here we are again—God doesn't show up in my life like he does in other people's lives.

Why?

Because you're scum, Brandon.

As Nashville Predators fans charmingly chant to opposing goalies after scoring against them:

"You suck. It's all your fault. It's all your fault."

You're the reason there's no power.

You're the reason there's no money.

You're the reason the church is flailing.

You're the bad one, Brandon.

EMPTY HANDED

After that experience I found myself broken, depressed, and spiritually numb. I was really angry at God because I knew I'd done everything right—I'd followed the plan.

He was the one who hadn't bothered to do his part.

It was around this time that "Love Wins" came out—you know, that horrible, dangerous book by that earlier mentioned man to whom we've since bid farewell.

And I was on board.

But get this ...

I came to the belief that God was so good, so loving, and so forgiving that he would literally forgive every single person who ever lived ... And yet, he still didn't like *me*.

That Christmas, kind of on a whim, my wife bought me Beauty Will Save the World by Brian Zahnd. I started reading it few weeks later and I could not, for the life of me, figure it out.

What was this guy saying?

Was he some sort of liberal charlatan?

He kept talking about violence and the Sermon on the Mount and how Evangelicalism was too closely aligned with American political agendas ...

I literally had no clue how to wrap my mind around it—and he was using language I'd heard in church for thirty years.

So I did what anyone would do—I looked him up on YouTube.

I watched an older message of his called A Beautiful Gospel, and in this message, he talks about how if Jesus is God, Jesus would show us what God is like. Brian would say, "God is like Jesus. God has always been like Jesus. We haven't always known this, but now we do."

So when the woman caught in adultery is brought before Jesus, and the religious people challenge him on what to do—you know, *because the Bible says we should stone her*—Jesus sends them away, telling her that he does not condemn her.

As Brian noted, we don't ever see Jesus turning people away because of their flaws, because of their humanness. He ate with the "sinners," got drunk with them, hung out with prostitutes, and healed the hearts of those wrestling with demons.

In fact, the only people who turned human beings away in the gospel narratives were the Pharisees.

And that was the biggest moment in my "re-construction"—it dawned on me that *I had been chasing after the approval of a cosmic Pharisee my entire life.*

Because the Pharisees condemned her to death, but **God** did not condemn at all.

And she didn't have to do a thing.

She didn't have to clean up her act.

She didn't have to grovel for forgiveness.

God hadn't condemned her in the first place.

I realized at that moment that if God was real, he must be like Jesus, and that Jesus was someone who would like me—he'd want to grab a beer with me at Fleet Street Pub and watch Arsenal, God's chosen football club.

Because I wasn't scum to the God who looks like Jesus.

And I didn't have to earn her favor.

I'd never lost it.

It was during this message that, for the first time in my life, I opened my fists.

And saw that *my hands were empty.*

There was nothing there.

All this time, I had been clutching air.

I slowly began to understand that with open hands, palms up, I could actually receive something, enjoy humanity, and simply be loved.

I could have stayed on the path, clutching at ozone, but I would have lost my faith.

Instead, I opened my fists and walked away.

And it saved my soul.

REPENTANCE

So where did that land me?

It's led me to a holistic faith that I hold with open hands, rather than clenched fists.

Because (shrugs shoulders) I could be wrong.

But I do believe that if there is a God, he looks like Jesus.

And I believe that our understanding of God is stilted if it's boiled down to a legal transaction, a question of "if you died tonight …"

So no more bronze aged child sacrifice.

No more condemnation of people with different beliefs or no beliefs at all.

No more Bible verse karate to prove how right I am.

No more believing that my daughters (or anyone else) are inherently depraved.

No more thinking that one political party is good and the other is evil.

No more bitterness for where other people are on their journey.

No more pressure to conform.

No more believing that I'm scum.

And God, it feels great.

I have never been so free in my life.

Free to reconsider points of view when I'm presented with new information.

Free to love people without coercing them to a particular way of thinking.

Free to teach my daughters that God will always love them no matter what, that their dad will always love them no matter what, and that kindness is magic.

Free to advocate for people who have done horrible things.

Free to believe that which resonates with my soul without trying to possess it.

Free to see the good in people, even when they hurt me.

Free to rest and create and risk and hope.

And most satisfyingly, I'm free to call bullshit when I see it.

So if any part of my journey sounds familiar, I'd say keep going.

Clear out all the mental furniture and burn some sage in the room of your mind.

Be angry because you were let down by the cosmic Pharisee and others.

It's okay, she can handle it.

So rage, cry, and shake your fists.

Then open up them and receive whatever it is that comes to you.

It may look completely different than my experience, but I'd be willing to bet it's better than where you've been. That's not to say it will be easy, but you will be free to accept whatever gifts life offers with open hands.

Written exclusively for this book by Brandon Dragan, 2021.

10

FINALLY BECOMING WHO WE'VE ALWAYS BEEN

JASON ELAM

Twice in my life, I have been overwhelmed by the white-hot love of God. Those two encounters were thirty years, a twenty-year career in local church ministry, an abusive marriage, divorce, and scandalous remarriage apart. The first encounter launched me into my spiritual evolution. The second probably saved my life and undoubtedly saved my faith.

My introduction to the Christian faith came at the age of seven at a children's revival held at our large Church of the Nazarene near Dayton, Ohio. Instead of the normal old white guy in a suit telling us what God had to say, a Children's revival meant that we kids got to listen to a different old white guy in a suit—and his wife! These folks brought puppets so I thought it was the best church service I had ever attended in my life. After the puppet show, the kindly old reverend very sweetly told us that we were sinners and that God can't look upon sin. Because God was so disgusted by the sight of us, He had to murder somebody to punish them for all of the wickedness in our hearts. God's chosen form of execution turned out to be a flaming pit where all of us sinners would burn for all eternity. Seeing this inevitable fate approaching, Jesus (God's only good Son) volunteered to come and die so the rest of delinquents didn't have to burn in hell as long as we would get baptized, go to church, read the Bible every day, pray, not cuss, not drink, not smoke, not have sex outside of marriage, and not listen to secular music. I'm sure all of those specific sins weren't implicitly mentioned in that particular sermon, but the impression that I got that night was that I was disgusting, God wanted to punish me, and I needed to go down to the front of the church that night to apologize to God for what a horrible sinner I was and beg Him to cover me with the blood of Jesus so He could forget how disgusting I really was. As I went forward that night, I prayed, I cried, I confessed everything I could think of, and I promised God I would try hard to do better. Shortly after that night, I was baptized.

The damage was done. The moment we buy into the lie that we have to fear the One who created us a wall is built that is so difficult to scale. A fear-based relationship with God made me constantly insecure. No effort on my part would ever be good enough, but I kept trying. I tried for years. During my teenage years whenever I'd slip up, I'd beg God to forgive me. I'd promise to do better only to slip up again. It was a self-fulfilling cycle of failure, confession, repentance, renewed effort, and more failure.

As an adolescent with a chronic sore throat, I went into the hospital for a routine tonsillectomy. During the surgery, I had a reaction to the anesthesia that stopped my heart on the operating table. During that lifeless period, I saw the cliché light radiating from the end of the tunnel and felt myself strangely drawn to the light. The closer I got to the light, the more I could see that the light was emanating from a person. In this person's presence, I felt completely known, accepted, and loved and I knew that nothing that I ever did would change that. I also felt a deep sense that my life mattered, that I had nothing to prove to anyone, and that my time on earth was not yet at an end. As I woke up from the surgery, I thought it had all been some crazy, drug-induced dream. Then I heard my Mom talking to one of her best friends on the phone about how they had lost me during the surgery but the doctor's had thankfully been able to resuscitate me.

You would think that after an experience like that, I would never doubt God's love for me again, but fear and legalism had already done their damage. That's the problem with religion—it injects us with just enough truth that we are inoculated against genuine good news. While I was confident in God's love for me, I was convinced that I now had a responsibility to somehow "live up to it". Years later, this would ultimately manifest in me "answering the call" to vocational ministry.

Because there was still so much fear and insecurity in my heart, my preaching became a vehicle through which I could receive the validation that I so desperately craved. I quickly learned that people in Alabama's Bible Belt (where I was living at that time) equated fire and brimstone preaching with anointing from God. I would passionately proclaim God's holiness, humanity's sinfulness, and the cure of putting your faith in the blood of Jesus to cleanse you from your filthy ways. My success or failure was directly tied to how many people stepped forward at the end of the service to give their hearts to Jesus.

I was the preacher that pastors would bring in when their congregations had fallen into loose living or started asking too many uncomfortable questions. I would come in and dismantle a congregation's sense of righteousness and convince the whole lot of them that they were filthy sinners desperately lacking the holiness that God demanded. People would stream to the front. Occasionally, even church leaders would come forward to give their hearts to Jesus after one of my burdensome guilt trips. The response was never enough to purge my insecurity.

After years of serving as an itinerant minister, I settled into a role as a youth pastor, then later an associate pastor, and ultimately became a senior pastor. People quickly became exhausted with my impossible standards and weekly guilt trips and the churches I served generally declined quickly. Desperate to overcome this perceived failure, I would turn to God with marathon scripture reading sessions, hours of prayer, and periods of fasting. Fasting was something that boosted my own sense of spiritual superiority and made me even more difficult to tolerate as a preacher. When that still didn't turn the church around, I desperately went for a walk in the woods behind our church to clear my head and try to figure out what to do. Every time I took that walk, Jesus met me there. I didn't see Him physically, but I sensed His presence and heard His voice. I would ask my endless questions seeking answers about how to save my fledgling church, but He didn't seem to have any interest in discussing that. He just wanted me to know how loved and accepted I was—exactly as I already was. I would talk endlessly about all of the ways I had failed to live up to the example He had set and been unworthy of His love, but He would just keep reminding me that His love had never been dependent upon my behavior. That was contrary to everything I had believed about God, so I would go back to the Bible and talk myself out of believing it. In those years I became fascinated with God's love and grace, but my messages became a double minded mix of God's mercy and wrath that left the listeners feeling hopelessly confused.

After years of trying to straddle the line between the love of God and the legalism in my own heart, I was exhausted, bitter, and physically depleted. My divorce had left me feeling disqualified from ministry and my quick remarriage had given my critics all the ammunition they needed to excommunicate me from the established religious circles in our area. Doors that had previously been open to me were now closed. In an effort to stay active in ministry, I started one non-denominational church after another. These churches were an experiment in creating a church for people who hate church. Folks who felt rejected and marginalized by the established churches in our area would come and we would commiserate together. Our focus was our pain. I was still preaching a muddled stream of grace and works that didn't provide a sense of peace for anyone so the results were the same. People would generally come for a few months only to leave a few months later.

The constant departures only fed my insecurity and made me more frustrated than ever. My health had begun to suffer as a result of the constant stress. Desperate, I started reading books by people outside of the scope of accepted Christian thought—Brad Jersak, William Paul Young, Sara Miles, and others. I began to see a vibrant faith outside of the limitations of my Bible Belt sensibilities. While I came to have a deep trust in the love of God, I held onto the conviction that most people were excluded from that love and that unless they accepted Jesus they would suffer in hell for eternity. I reassured myself that God wasn't sending them there, but that they were choosing it for themselves.

One day, I was walking around the circular track at my local gym. As I walked, I listened to a new podcast hosted by writer Jonathan Martin called "Son of a Preacher Man". On this particular episode, Martin was interviewing his friend, Brad Jersak, and they were discussing the depth of God's love. I wish I could explain what happened to me that day. Words absolutely fail me. The best that I can come up with is that it felt like waves of liquid love were crashing over me as I walked the track-every wave washing away years of fear and rejection. Tears of joy streamed down my face. I'm sure people in the gym that day thought I was having some sort of breakdown—and maybe I was. Right there in the gym, I had run headfirst into the same loving presence I had encountered while dead on the operating table decades earlier. I was again known, accepted, and loved with nothing to prove to anyone. But this was no drug induced dream. For the first time in my life, I was wide awake.

When I got on the track that day, I believed most of humanity would suffer for eternity in hell having fallen short of the glory of God. When I left the gym that day, I believed that the love of God was big enough to include every human being who had ever lived and ever will. I knew that all were welcome at the table of

Jesus-even those who deny His existence. For me personally, I knew that my value didn't depend on anything that I did. The success or failure of my ministry did not determine my worth. I was free to finally lay down the expectations of those around me and finally be at peace with who I had always been. I could finally be who I had always been.

I wish I could tell you that I have been able to live in that sacred reality every day since, but that would be a lie. Insecurity and fear still have way too much control in my life. But every day, I believe more and more in the love of a God whose only agenda for me is to know how deeply loved I am.

I also wish I could say that everyone around me was as excited as I was about my newfound faith in God's universal love. As I voiced my new conviction, several trusted friends walked away. Our church struggled financially as many of the donors who had kept it afloat didn't want anything to do with me anymore. The precious few who stuck around joined in with my wife, kids, and I as we set out in a new direction. Since our church was in one of the poorest communities in Alabama, we decided to ask the community what they needed. They told us they needed food. So we converted our little chapel into a free indoor farmer's market helping people struggling financially get the food they needed for themselves and their families. The presence of God filled that place as hungry people experienced love without any agenda whatsoever. We gave away food until the money ran out and the church finally closed for good.

Today, worship looks more like teaching my son to ride his bike, checking in on my parents, long car rides with my daughter, or sunsets at the beach with my incredible wife, Brandi.

As decades of active local church ministry came to an end, I experienced real and lasting peace. I no longer feel the need to prove myself to anyone. I am fully known and fully loved and free to love others without expecting anything whatsoever in return. And so are you.

I'm not anyone to give advice. I've been wrong about so many things over the years. I have heaped hellfire, damnation, shame, fear, and unworthiness onto the lives of thousands of people and nothing that I do from here on out will ever change that. I'm at peace, but I live with regret for all those who were hurt by my preaching.

I want to leave you with one thought. As our spiritual evolution takes us into unfamiliar territory outside of mainstream Christian thought, there we will be well-intentioned (and perhaps some not so well-intentioned) friends and family members who fear for our souls and call us to return to the faith of our upbringing-but there is nothing for us there. As our legalism, shame, and fear are stripped away, we can experience real peace that isn't dependent upon meeting the expectations of anyone around us. In those times, it can be hard to articulate the freedom you've found. Some may try to challenge you with scripture, their favorite doctrine, or a download of a sermon from their favorite preacher. When that happens, I hope you will remember that you are fully known, loved, and accepted exactly as you are and that you don't have to live up to the expectations of anyone around you in order to be at peace. God doesn't love us because we have all of our beliefs in order. God just loves us because that's who God is.

You have come from love.

You live in love.

You are held by love.

You are returning to love.

Your inherent nature is good.

You can trust the leading of your own heart.

You are free to finally become the person you've always been.

You are more loved than you can possibly imagine and God is closer to you than your next breath.

So breathe—and be at peace.

Written exclusively for this book by Jason Elam, 2021.

11

WHAT'S SEX GOT TO DO WITH IT? MAYBE EVERYTHING

REV. DR. KATY VALENTINE

Religious deconstruction is hard enough, but throw sex and gender into the mix? It is a head-spinning, body-gripping cocktail of confusion. The messages of conservative evangelical Christian culture that you may be questioning include:

- Men are the 'head of the household' and women are complementary partners
- Sex is for marriage only and only between one man and one woman

- The only correct and only acceptable sexual orientation is heterosexual
- Homosexuality is curable, in both practice and thoughts
- Other sexual orientations do not really exist
- The only legitimate gender identities are "man" and "woman," and transgender persons are confused
- Women need purity codes to keep them chaste and virginal before marriage

Conservative evangelicalism promises that these values keep an orderly (if boring) household. To some degree, this is true, and the hierarchical structure does have a certainty to it that may be comforting to some. Unfortunately, this structure is really only a façade of orderliness. In reality, it creates mental and emotional stress, especially for those not at the top of the household. The myth is that a young, heterosexual couple falls in love and gets married, having magical sex for the first time on their wedding night. They form a household with a few children, and the orderliness of the husband as the head of the household and a submissive (yet opinionated) wife keeps the household running like clockwork. Occasional disagreements may occur, but everything will be put right again because of the faithfulness of maintaining the hierarchical structure.

The reality of course is that life is much messier. The hierarchy that promises order usually only creates resentment and challenges, though often unspoken for years or even decades. Some couples have difficulty achieving intimacy, and a very non-magical wedding night turns into years of challenging sexual intimacy. Many women experience shame and guilt over any sexual contact at all, even after marriage. Feelings of desire by either spouse for the same sex may be repressed for years, often accompanied by dire coping mechanisms, including addiction and violent behavior. Children who are gay or trans may be unable to tell parents for fear of judgment or even safety, continuing a cycle of depression and addiction. When people are unable to become their full authentic selves, the soul suffers. The orderliness promised by purity culture and the sexual ethos of conservative evangelical religion is a myth; it cannot be achieved by faithful Christians. The truth is that people cannot thrive under such limiting values of human sexuality and gender.

Now for the good news! The Spirit constantly calls us to re-create ourselves. The twin topics of sexuality and gender are among the most challenging to deconstruct. Fortunately, the emerging questions and opportunities to form new ideas, while challenging, can also be fun—yes, fun!—because we get to be playful, sometimes for the first time, around about our own sense of sex and gender. To be sure, sexual and gender identities are powerful motivators in our human lives. Because these identities involve our own bodies and most intimate relationships, they carry added emotional weight. It may take a bit of time and re-orienting to gain the freedom of a new vision of sexuality and gender, and it is worth the effort.

This article is divided into several sections to assist you in the process of deconstructing and reconstructing ideas around sexuality and gender. First is an exploration of Scripture with an exploration of the idea that just one model of sexuality is incorrect. Then I turn briefly to the topics of sex, gender and gender identity, and sexual orientation. Each topic addresses the myths that deconstruction process can dismantle, options for reconstruction, and a resource to assist you on the journey. Plus, I'll share some of my journey along the way—and hopefully a jump start a bit of fun to get you started on your own journey.

SCRIPTURE

Deconstruction Process: What does the Bible say about sex? A lot, actually. I used to joke with my undergraduates that in order to read the Bible, they would need to get *real* comfortable with a lot of sex and a lot of talk about circumcision. Scripture interestingly does not shy away from sex *at all*. Written in a time when life spans were short and birth control was unavailable, the frank talk about sex in the Bible reflects a concern with continuing familial lines in uncertain times. The myth that you are invite to deconstruct is this: Scripture only approves of a particular sexual ethic such as "no sex before marriage" or "women's virginity is owned by their fathers."

The truth is far more interesting and compelling, which is that the Bible has a diversity of images of sexuality.

It may be helpful to have an option to reframe the conservative evangelical interpretation of Scripture regarding sexuality. Even with this diversity, most, if not all, of Scripture all reflect a *patriarchal structure*. This patriarchal structure was embedded in the ancient world, and it celebrated female chastity while championing male virility (sound familiar?). While you are considering your own questions to ask about Scripture, it may be helpful to consider that the patriarchal structure of the Bible is less of a divine mandate than a reflection of human culture that shaped the writing of Scripture. Conservative evangelical culture has taken this myth and spun it into an absolute truth. Still, even with this patriarchal structure, views of sexuality that go against the grain are apparent in Scripture.

Reconstruction Options: This diversity is most apparent in the Song of Songs (sometimes called the Song of Solomon). This book is about young lovers who are unmarried unmarried yet passionately engaging in sex.

> *let us go out early to the vineyards,*
>   *and see whether the vines have budded,*
> *whether the grape blossoms have opened*
>   *and the pomegranates are in bloom.*
> *There I will give you my love*

– SONG OF SOLOMON 7:12

Or even more directly:

> *My beloved thrust his hand into the opening,*
>   *and my inmost being yearned for him*

– SONG OF SOLOMON 5:4

While many evangelical youth are taught that the verse "do not stir up or awaken love until it is ready" (Song of Solomon 3:5) is a mandate to wait until marriage to have sex, this is a weak attempt to force the text to fit into a purity culture model. In the text, the young woman is *more* than ready to experience the delights of sensuality and sex. The Song of Solomon celebrates this love with passion and vigor.[75]

Other biblical stories also show sexuality in ways that do not subscribe to a purity culture model, such as the Bible's widespread acceptance of prostitution as a legitimate way for a woman without means to make a living. In the story of Judah and Tamar in Genesis 38, and the story of the two prostitutes who come before King Solomon in 1 Kings 3:16-38, prostitution is merely accepted as a fact without condemnation of the women involved. Polygamy is widespread throughout the Hebrew Scriptures, including the parents of the prophet Samuel (1 Samuel 1:1-2). Paul advocated celibacy and only wished for people to marry as a last resort if they could not control their sexual desire (1 Cor 7:2-5), an option which many early Christian women took advantage of and refused to marry, also avoiding the dangers of childbirth in the ancient world. This short list shows that there is no *one* way that Scripture portrays sexuality or even a sexual ethic. It is inappropriate to select one and only one as "the" model for human sexuality. Imagine if we took only recommendations of Paul as the basis for marriage today— very few people would get married, and those who did would only do so for the purposes of sexual satisfaction but not for love or companionship. Scripture provides us options rather than models.

Simply the realization that portrayals of sexuality exist in Scripture may be shocking. The freedom that comes with this search in Scripture can be compelling, even while confusing. Sexuality is less of a fixed factor in human life, and more of a continuous development across the human life span. As you are considering your own response to deconstructing sexuality, do any of these Scripture stories spark an interest for you? Which ones would you like to explore more to get a well-founded view of sexuality in Scripture?

---

75. The interpretation of the Song of Solomon has been that the lovers in the book represent the love of Christ for the Church in Christianity or God's love for Israel in Judaism. While these interpretations seem far-fetched today, I am grateful for them because they kept this book in the biblical canon.

Resource: The book *Unprotected Texts* by Jennifer Knust is a fascinating look at sexuality in the Bible, and she explores numerous stories and options for unpacking sexuality for a contemporary believer.[76]

SEX: WHAT DO I DO NOW?

Deconstruction Process: With the wide ranging-depictions of sexuality in the Bible, what about sex, specifically sexual intercourse and sexual partners? This might be the moment where the deconstruction process can feel overwhelming. The myth to deconstruct around sex is that a purity model offers fulfilling promises for marriage and sex within marriage. The purity model is one that keeps young people, especially women, sexually pure prior to marriage. This means no sex and limited physical sexual contact prior to marriage. This myth presumes that a woman's sexuality is owned or guarded by her father and then transferred to her husband. comfort because everything is laid out in a neat, orderly way. This myth has been busted in recent studies that have shown how this model produces mental and emotional distress, especially for women.[77] The overwhelming messages that sex is dirty and that the body, especially the female body, is a source of temptation takes a toll on both the body and the psyche. The body, which should be a source of joy and delight as incarnated beings, instead becomes a focus of shame. Many women after marriage report painful sex, emotionally disconnected sex, and the inability to have sex at all. Many people feel pressured into marriage at a young age for the sole purpose of

76. Jennifer Knust, *Unprotected Texts: The Bible's Surprising Contradictions about Sex and Desire*, New York: Harper Collins, 2011.

77. For a critique and analysis of purity culture, see Sara Moslener, *Virgin Nation: Sexual Purity and American Adolescence*, Oxford: Oxford University Press, 2015. See the recent study written by and for evangelical women, Sheila Wray Gregoire, Rebecca Gregoire LIndenbach and Joanna Sawatsky, *The Great Sex Rescue: The Lies You've Been Taught and How to Recover What God Intended*, Grand Rapids: Baker Books, 2021.

being able to experience sexual intercourse, and they find as they mature that the decision may be been premature.

My own process of untangling purity culture messages offers a glimpse into its damaging afterlife. After I had sex for the first time, I worried for months that I might have gotten HIV. Logically, I knew that I had engaged in safe sex, but the lingering effects of an evangelical culture that stressed purity and warned against pre-marital sex with dire warnings of disease, shame, and a stained soul was strong. My body stored up a lot of the messages that I had received, and it became expressed in this fixated worry. It would take several more years of shifting my awareness and patience for my body and internalized messages to catch up with my head.

Fast forward several years, and when I moved in with a partner with whom I was in a committed relationship but without plans to marry, my parents exploded. Months followed of silent treatments coupled with begging and pleading and injunctions to "get on my knees and pray." Though my parents had rejected the rigidity of their own evangelical upbringing, the messages around sexuality and purity continued to linger and were passed on to me in a harm-ful, though well-intentioned, manner. In a way, all three of us were caught in a loop of purity culture madness and damage. (We get along great now; this was a serious but ultimately good learning curve for all of us).

Reconstruction Options: If the model of sexual purity before mar-riage does not hold up as *the* model, and certainly not one that promotes healthy emotional, mental, and physical well-being, then what are the possibilities? A healthy cautionary note here is that every exploration *has to feel safe and resonant with the individual who is exploring.* This is not a suggestion that everyone launch into a libertine, free love lifestyle (though you can if you want—be sure to educate yourself first). It is simply the opportunity to try on differ-ent ways of being sexual that are supportive to the reconstruction process. Perhaps you are single, or even newly divorced, and won-dering what responsible sexuality may look like for you. Or perhaps you are happily married and you and your spouse are deconstruct-ing together. It could also be that you are married or partnered and that you are deconstructing but your spouse is not. Wherever you are on this journey, it is *your journey*, and only you can determine the best sexual ethic for you.

A healthy first step can be to normalize new values around sex. Eventually, these can replace some of the old values that cause emotional distress. Try on these statements and see how they fit for you:

- Sexual desire is normal and healthy
- Consensual sex outside of marriage is a choice to be made by the individual; it is not "right" or "wrong" but simply an experience[78]
- Each person owns their own sexuality and has the right to determine their own sexual experiences (in other words, fathers do not own the sexuality of daughters, and husbands do not own the sexuality of wives)
- Negative past sexual experiences do not make up the totality of a person
- All sex should be consensual and contain the possibility of joy

In developing your own sexual ethic, a few pointers may be helpful. Continue to cultivate the awareness that Scripture is diverse on its expressions of sexual activity. You also have the right to go as slowly as you need to while you deconstruct what you used to know and begin to build your own vision of what sexual ethics apply to you. The sexual ethic you develop *must be in resonance with your values.*

Resource: The resource to share with you is an exercise that many people in my groups have found to be empowering. This is especially helpful when experiencing shame, anger, or resentment from past messaging around purity and sex. These emotions have a way of living deep in the body, but they can be released from the body and psyche. This exercise is one that helps locate where the

---

78. This statement specifically refers to those who are single; I do not say "before marriage" because that implies that marriage is for everyone and a "goal" in life. This statement is not speaking about illicit affairs within marriage.

emotions reside and begin to address them one at a time. A huge benefit of this exercise is that it gets us out of the story that the emotions are telling and gets us into the present so where we can try on new beliefs.

The exercise is quite simple, but powerful. When any emotion like shame, anger, or resentment arise, simply note where it is occurring in your body. Does the heart feel tight? Or the head feel confused? Perhaps the low belly feels rigid and tight? Wherever this response is within your body, you are invited to place a hand on it and simply breathe with awareness that your body has been holding on to this feeling for a long time. Name the emotion (anger, shame, embarrassment, etc.). Acknowledging the emotion has a way of letting it begin to release so that you can tell a new story. It is strange, but often true, that ignoring the emotion lets it linger on while acknowledging its presence allows it to begin to shift. Simply sit with this for a few minutes (often just 90 seconds is enough) until the feeling begins to lighten or shift a little bit. Avoid judging the feeling or experience; simply let it be. When done, you have the option of stating the *new* belief that you have out loud (such as "I believe that sex is God-given"). Repeat as often as necessary.

When any lingering negative feeling arises within me, especially around sexuality or gender, this exercise of placing a hand on the part of the body where it is felt and simply acknowledging it almost always allows it to start to shift. If this exercise produces additional anxiety, of course, then it may not be for you. Many people have found this to be an effective way of comforting themselves and of getting reacquainted with the body in an empowering way. By placing our hand on our bodies, we are telling ourselves that we see our created bodies as *good* and worthy of this positive attention.

GENDER AND GENDER IDENTITY

Deconstruction: Messages around gender are particularly thorny. In consideration of the genders that we call "men" and "women," the conservative evangelical message is *complementarian*. This is a mythic belief that men and women *complement* one another but have distinct roles and authority within the household. In other words, it is a myth of 'separate but equal' (which does not work) that puts women in a space of continuous repressed anger and sometimes shame. Biblical passages are misinterpreted or selected in isolation to support this view as a God-ordained one that takes women out of decision-making and leadership. Furthermore, womanhood becomes synonymous with *motherhood*, a damaging stereotype for both men and women. Similar toxic messages exist around masculinity and men's roles, but the damage for women runs deep, affecting women's self-esteem and upward mobility.

Another myth around gender in evangelical dogma is that gender is *fixed* and determined solely by biological sex. To put it simply, infants born with a penis become men (thus head of the household), and infants born with a vagina become women (complementary to men). This message equates gender roles with biology and does not allow for any fluidity of gender expression or identity. Denying the fluidity of gender, especially for transpersons, is toxic and leads to high rates of self-harm and suicide. Shifting from a perspective of gender as *fixed* to *fluid* is a challenging component of deconstruction, and one that is worth your time and energy.

Reconstruction: Dismantling the idea that gender, and gender roles, are not fixed can be liberating. Just as Scripture does not have one view of sexuality, it also does not have one view of gender. Women like Miriam and Deborah are presented as leaders and not evaluated in Scripture in terms of the limitations of their gender (hint: there are none!), and these women are not evaluated in terms of being mothers. Huldah prophesies in the temple directly to high priests and indirectly to King Josiah about the "book of the law" that was discovered. As mentioned above, many women in the early church chose to remain celibate, taking charge of their own sexuality, avoiding motherhood and childbearing. These examples offer multiple examples of women's roles and authority, and they may even suggest that no one model of gender is needed; women, and men, can determine for themselves how they want to exercise leadership within the household and church.

The discussion of gender does not end with only women's roles in Scripture and in church and household today. Gender is far more encompassing than only male/female or men/women. *Gender identity* is an important topic to consider, especially with new awareness around gender identities such as transgender or gender non-conforming and how these relate to biological sex. As you can imagine, Scripture does speak with one voice about the relationship between biological sex and gender. A few definitions may be helpful here:

Biological sex: The sex at birth of an infant, determined (usually) by external sex organs. Many acknowledge only two sexes, male and female, but this fails to take into account intersex, or those who are born with both male and female sex organs.

Gender identity: The identity of a person based on their internal sense of their gender (independent of their biological sex).

Most people who are born male grow up to identify as men, and most people who are born female grow up to identify as women, but there is growing awareness that many people do not identify their *gender* with their *biological sex*. In a way, though, this makes a lot of sense. If gender roles do not actually exist as divinely ordained, then why should something as arbitrary as biology determine someone's gender? Gender identity is the gender that someone has *independent of their biological sex*. Cisgender persons are those people for whom their gender identity and biological sex match. Transgender persons are those people whose gender identity and biological sex do not align in the expected way. For instance, a transman is someone who is born with female genitalia but identifies as a man. A transwoman is someone who is born with male genitalia but identifies as a woman. A host of other gender identities exist as well, such as agender (no gender) or genderqueer (non-binary and does not identify exclusively as man or woman). The major point here is that biology does not have to determine our gender identity.

In my own journey, the idea of gender roles felt stifling. I met any number of women as a teen who told me that their husband as the "head of the household" was needed when there was a final decision to be made in the household, even though their input was valued as a complementary member of the house. This separate but equal status never gave full autonomy or authority to the women in the household or in their church life. It was common in my family to go to my grandmother's after church to have Sunday lunch. The women would labor in the kitchen, and the men would watch sports. I protested but was generally silenced and told that the "men work so hard during the week" (believe me, the women were working equally as hard in both paid and unpaid labor). The visibility of these gender roles enacted directly after a church service gave them a quasi-seal of religious approval.[79]

I emerged from these expected gender roles into my own sense of my own power and authority slowly over the years. I sought relationships where my partner and I matched one another as autonomous adults making joint decisions. Whenever someone tries to pigeonhole me now according to marital or maternal status, I am able to offer a gentle (or not so gentle) corrective; I am complete by myself without fulfilling any pre-determined roles.

In my scholarship as a New Testament scholar, I explore not only gender roles but *gender identity*, specifically transgender identity. Many transgender Christians have offered me their stories and insights about Scripture and their own gender journey, and I have been grateful to the churches that have opened their doors to radical inclusion and working to undo prescribed gender roles. One of the formative passages in the Bible that points to the multiplicity of gender is found right at the beginning in Genesis 1:26-27:

Then God said, 'Let us make humankind in our image, according to our likeness ...

79. This is meant with no disrespect of my pastors growing up, most of whom I believe would also protest such gender roles. The culture in which I was embedded, though, promoted binary gender roles and treated any difference with suspicion. My family did not operate under extreme oppression (my mom did all of the finances in the household), but often it's the subtle signals around gender that are long lasting.

So God created humankind in his image,
in the image of God he created them;
male and female he created them.

Sometimes these verses are used to solidify gender roles, but a closer look at them indicates the delightful variety that God has given humans regarding gender. God is self-referential here using "us" and "our" rather than "me" or a pronoun such as "he" or "her." This is a curious feature in the text; many Christians often assume that this is a trinitarian conversation, but I find it much more compelling to see these verses as a recognition that God's own Being is multi-gendered. When humankind is created in God's image, they are created both male and female, reflecting God's own nature. Some ancient interpreters assumed that the first human being was an androgyne, containing both male and female sexual organs in one being. Perhaps the story oints to the fact that even God's own self cannot be contained or defined by a gender—and neither can ours, since we are made in the image of God.[80]

Resource: The Christian Church (Disciples of Christ) has a ministry, Alliance Q, that works for greater equality and inclusion of members of the LGBTQ+ community. Their resources on transgender and Christianity are helpful (including a video of a sermon that I gave in 2016): http://disciplesallianceq.org/resources-category/transgender/

SEXUAL ORIENTATION

Deconstruction Process: Sexual orientation has become a litmus test for religious groups in recent years, and conservative evangelicals have landed for the most part in the camp that rejects anything other than a heterosexual orientation. The myth to deconstruct

80. I wrote a recent article on transgender interpretations if Genesis 1:26-27; see Katy E. Valentine, "Examining Scripture in Light of Trans Women's Voices," pages 509–24 in *The Oxford Handbook of Feminist Approaches to the Hebrew Bible*. Edited by Susanne Scholz. Oxford: Oxford University Press, 2021.

around sexual orientation is that homosexuality and bisexuality are wrong, or that they are something to be cured. "Homosexual" refers to people who are attracted to their same sex (men attracted to men; women attracted to women) while "heterosexual" refers to people attracted to the "opposite" sex (men attracted to women; women attracted to men). "Bisexual" refers to someone who is attracted to both men and women. The condemnation of same sex attraction has been a painful process for gay, lesbian, and bisexual Christians, their families and friends, and detrimental to communities as a whole. For those who have been presented with idea that the only legitimate way to feel sexual desire is to that of the "opposite" sex, it can be a rewarding process to begin the journey towards greater inclusion and understanding.[81]

Reconstruction: This topic is a challenging one for a lot of people who are deconstructing their faith precisely because it has become a hot button issue in recent decades. Sometimes even exploring the world behind the "clobber texts" that are used to condemn homosexuality within conservative evangelical churches can bring up such anxiety that it is challenging to engage.[82] Many resources exist to assist in understanding these verses, their origins, and what they

---

81. In fact, even the term "opposite sex" may not make a lot of sense in light of the discussion around gender identity—why are men and women viewed as "opposite" from one another? Once the door cracks open to exploring sexuality and gender, the terms get harder to define—and this is a good thing. God is too abundant for the limitations of only two genders.

82. Genesis 19:1-38; Leviticus 18:22, 20:13; Romans 1:25-27; 1 Corinthians 6:9-11; 1 Timothy 1:9-10; Jude 6-7.

actually mean that readers can go through in their own time.[83] For now, it may be helpful to consider the diversity of sexual and gender expressions that appear on what we call a *spectrum*.

In recent years, we have come to understand that sexual orientation and attraction exist on *a spectrum*. In fact, many other sexual orientations exist other than "heterosexual" and "homosexual." While these two orientations have been held up as polar ends of a spectrum, it is more accurate to visualize the spectrum as 3D rather than a straight (forgive the pun) line. For instance, other sexual orientations include:

- Bisexual: attraction to both men and women
- Pansexual: attracted to all gender identities
- Demisexual: attracted only to people when there is a romantic feeling
- Asexual: does not experience sexual attraction at all (but may experience romantic attraction)

The focus on "homosexual" vs. "heterosexual" in evangelical conservatism is ultimately about control of sexuality—but, ironically, it is also short sighted. Sexual orientation is only one of the many spectrums within the human experience of sexuality and gender. Other spectrums include gender expression (how we dress and express our gender), romantic attraction (distinct from sexual attraction), emotional attraction (with whom we share our deepest emotional connections), and probably other spectrums as well. For instance, someone might be transwoman who was assigned male at birth. Her gender expression might be androgynous to a little

83. To get a sense of the "clobber passages" in their original context, check out *Homosexuality, Science, and the "Plain Sense" of Scripture*. Edited by David L. Balch. Grand Rapids: Eerdmans, 1999. For queer friendly interpretations of Scripture, check out *Bible Trouble: Queer Reading at the Boundaries of Biblical Scholarship*. Edited by Theresa J. Hornsby and Ken Stone. Atlanta: Society of Biblical Literature, 2011; Tonyia M. Rawls, "Yes, Jesus Loves Me: The Liberating Power of Spiritual Acceptance for Black Lesbian, Gay, Bisexual and Transgender Christians," pages 327-52 in *Black Sexualities: Probing Powers, Passions, Practices, and Policies*. Edited by Juan Battle and Sanra L. Barnes. New Brunswick, NJ: Rutgers University Press, 2010.

feminine, and her sexual orientation might be to men while her romantic attraction might be to men and women; her emotional connection might be primarily with women but occasionally with men. All of these components are on a series of spectrums.

Understanding *all* of sexuality and gender as existing on many spectrums may help serve the reconstruction of the previous condemnation of those who identify as gay, lesbian, or bisexual. The great diversity that exists among human beings in this regard is a gift. If we were all the same, it would be a boring creation. Fortunately, God has given us a tapestry of diverse orientations, genders, and expressions. These, in turn, help us better understand who God is as our Creator.

Resource: I cannot think of a better companion in the journey of shifting to a place of inclusivity around sexual orientation than the Gender Unicorn. Yes, you read that correctly! This is a tool in the form of a unicorn developed to help students understand the many spectrums that exist for gender and sexuality. You can visit their website to fill out an interactive unicorn (https://transstudent.org/gender/).

With this creative resource, you can begin to assess your own spectrum and be in dialogue with others who are willing to converse with you about theirs. The idea is that you place a marker along each spectrum in the categories of the unicorn so that you can visibly see your own unique gender spectrum through the friendly unicorn. Take some time and consider your own gender identity, gender expression, sex assigned at birth, physical attraction and emotional attraction.

WHAT IS NEXT?

What is next on your journey? Perhaps some of the information above has helped identify the painful points of deconstruction around sexuality and gender and given you a handle on what the options are for reconstruction. The myths that are promised by conservative evangelical culture have been identified, but the next part is entirely up to you. The reconstruction process does not have a roadmap, especially around gender and sexuality. It does have, though, an element of fun once we can begin to consider new ideas and see ourselves, and everyone else, on a spectrum of God's glorious creation of sexuality and gender. A thread throughout this chapter has been the role of Scripture it the deconstruction and reconstruction process. Rather than experience Scripture as a bludgeon, it is my hope that it has the capacity to become a life affirming tool that gives you *options* for exploring sexuality and gender. What are the next steps? You decide.

Written exclusively for this book by Rev. Dr. Katy Valentine, 2021.

12

JOBIAN THEOLOGY

DERRICK DAY

I'd like to take on a subject that has silently taken over a large portion of mainstream Christianity: Jobian Theology.

Jobian theology comes from the premise that what happened to Job is greater than the finished work of Christ. Now, no Christian would ever admit to subscribing to such foolishness, but their words and deeds contradict this. By definition, a "Christian" is someone who aspires to be "like Christ." However, many "Christians" when evaluating their own lives and circumstances, see themselves more "like Job" than "like Christ," hence, "Jobians."

Job is the "poster boy" for religion. Whenever someone has to explain why bad things happen to good people, religious apologists run to Job.

First to level-set, the common assumption is that God granted permission to satan to afflict Job. Nothing could be further from the truth. First of all, God was not setting Job up to be knocked out-of-the-park by satan. The question in Job 1:8 "Have you considered my servant, Job," could be better translated "Hast thou set thine heart on," or "Hast thou given thine attention to." In other words, God was asking the devil why did he have his heart set on Job.

Satan saw the blessing on Job's life and thought Job served God only because he was blessed. In fact, satan's strategy was to get God to afflict Job. It is important to note here that when Job was afflicted, it was satan, and not God, who afflicted him.

Another thing to note is how satan approached God about this. He showed up at a time when the sons of God (angels) were gathering at the throne.

Now there was a day when the sons of God came to present themselves before the Lord, and Satan came also among them.

– JOB 1:6

He tried to conceal himself among the heavenly host. There's a lesson to be learned from this: that everyone among you isn't with you!

But back to the main point. The next point of consideration is that Job was operating in fear. Job continually offered sacrifices for his children, whom he suspected weren't living right:

And his sons went and feasted in their houses, every one his day; and sent and called for their three sisters to eat and to drink with them. And it was so, when the days of their feasting were gone about, that Job sent and sanctified them, and rose up early in the morning, and offered burnt offerings according to the number of them all: for Job said, It may be that my sons have sinned, and cursed God in their hearts. Thus did Job continually.

– JOB 1:4-5

The proof that Job was operating in fear was revealed later:

*For the thing which I greatly feared is come upon me, and that which
I was afraid of is come unto me*

– JOB 3:25

Nothing invites the devil into your situation more than fear.
Paul said it best in his second letter to Timothy:

*For God hath not given us the spirit of fear; but of power, and of love,
and of a sound mind*

– 2 TIMOTHY 1:17

I've said in prior treatises that faith is the currency of the
Kingdom of God. Conversely, fear is the currency of the principality of darkness. Job, like many Christians, today, failed to properly
exchange his currency. As a result, he brought the will, culture, and
intent of the principality of darkness into his world.

More to the point, Job was a man without a covenant. Job is
the oldest book in the Bible, chronologically speaking and Job had
neither the covenant of law nor the covenant of Grace. Job did not
have either Jesus or the indwelling of the Holy Spirit. This made
Job vulnerable, and it is proven when God makes a profound statement that has been terribly misinterpreted by theologians:

*And the Lord said unto Satan, Behold, all that he hath is in thy
power; only upon himself put not forth thine hand.*

– JOB 1:12

The challenge I pose here is, where is the permissive clause?
Where does God grant satan permission to afflict Job? Let me help
you, it ain't there. I've done a lot of searching and study on this,
and—as near as I can figure—whenever God says "behold," it is
usually followed by a truth. It is never used to grant permission to
do anything. Here are some examples:

*Behold, the Lord thy God hath set the land before thee: go up and
possess it, as the Lord God of thy fathers hath said unto thee; fear not,
neither be discouraged.*

– DEUTERONOMY 1:21

Therefore thus saith the Lord God, Behold, I lay in Zion for a foundation a stone, a tried stone, a precious corner stone, a sure foundation: he that believeth shall not make haste.

– ISAIAH 28:16

In both cases, a truth is stated but no permission is granted. In other words, what is stated in Job 1:12 ("Behold, all that he hath …") and in Job 2:6 ("Behold, he is in thine hand …") was not granting permission, it was stating a truth! It is critically important that this is seen because sin gave satan access to anyone outside covenant with God.

One thing that must be made abundantly clear, here, is that God did not grant satan access to Job—satan already had it! Job did not have a "hedge about him," that was satan's misunderstanding. However, God did raise a hedge around Job twice (Job 1:12 and 2:6) limiting what satan could do.

So, here's the million-dollar question, "Why didn't God stop all this?" Glad you asked. God can do anything but lie, fail, or violate His Word. The Psalmist tells us that God esteems His Word above His name (Psalm 138:2). Once God establish a thing by His Word, He will not do anything contrary to it. A great example of this is the concept of seedtime and harvest; God will not do anything contrary to this principle.

Another thing that must be clarified is that God is a good parent. Indeed, He is the most extraordinary of parents. As such, He will always do what is best for His children. That, said, would any good parent turn their child over to a known pervert to discipline them when they are out of order? Well, since God is the greatest parent and satan is the greatest pervert—in fact, he's the original pervert—God would not do that. It just doesn't add up. But God gave man dominion in the earth (Genesis 1:26-28)—dominion by which God expects us to influence our environment with His Word. Therefore, God didn't do anything about Job's situation because Job, himself, didn't do anything about his situation.

Whew. That was long winded—but I hope you caught it. If you didn't read it again (and again, if necessary) until you do!

One more thing: do you realize that God didn't actually chasten Job until near the end of the book? That's right, God didn't deal with Job until chapters 38-41—and when He did, did He heap more affliction upon Job? No, He chastened Job with His Word! This is consistent with 2 Timothy 3:16. In other words, the chastening for the child of God is the Word of God, not sickness, plague, oppression, pain, or poverty! And, at the end of God's chastening - and after Job repented (changed his mind) and prayed for his friends, God blessed Job with far more substance than what he had, before! Man, that is Good News!

If God afflicted Job then delivered Him, God acted against Himself—and since a kingdom divided cannot stand, God cannot be divided or double-minded! Jesus came to destroy the works of the devil and empower us to do likewise (1 John 3:8). God will not use the works of the devil to chasten and afflict His children when He already sent His Son to destroy those works!

Let me say this, God doesn't miss—He does what He says and says what He does. He is perfect in every way. However, He expects us to emulate Him. Also the Body of Christ is an interdependent vessel—every part is dependent upon other parts. In other words, the timely blessing of others may be contingent upon us being in the right place at the right time. So, when bad things happen to good people, it ain't God! Sometimes we miss it in what we pray for and decree. Other times we miss it when we miss an assignment. And, we must remember we live in a fallen world—and sometimes the devil uses the implements of this fallen world to thwart the prayers and actions of the Saints.

Bottom line, whose report will you believe? Will you trust in the finished work of Jesus, which gives us everything we need to experience abundant life (John 10:10) or will you place your trust in a statement that a mere man who suffered great loss without revelation of who stole from him (Job 1:21). Will you believe that God gives satan permission to afflict you, or will you trust that God will protect you (2 Thessalonians 3:3, 1 John 5:18). Will you trust the bondage of religion, or place your trust in the goodness of God?

In what and whom you believe determines whose you are—are you of Job or are you of Christ?

Adapted from the book, *Deconstructing Religion*, by Derrick Day, 2016.

13

RETHINKING EVANGELISM AND MISSIONS

SKEETER WILSON

THE SACRED COW

Education is one of the so-called achievements of missionaries that is touted in the article "The Surprising Discovery About Those Colonialist, Proselytizing Missionaries."

I will assume that most will agree with me that education is one of the West's most sacred cows. For the West, the theoretical purpose of education has been to maintain democracy. Since the industrial revolutions in the West, however, the practical purpose of education has become to produce a useful and compliant workforce (a discussion in itself). This motive has, in many ways, superseded all other motives. For a conversion Protestant, the additional and, in theory, greater purpose is to make it possible for everyone to be able to read the Bible in their own language.

Ultimately, the Western mind seems to believe that every problem can be solved with just a little more education—Western-style education, of course.

Every civilization has methods of education, some far more sophisticated than others, but education and its delivery is the essence of any civilization. If you kill the educational system of a culture, the culture will not survive. That statement should be uncontestable, or as the Puritans used to say, self-evident.

I will save until later some of the problems of the Western world's ideas of education and, more especially, the problem of education that is exported from one civilization to another. For now, however, let's stay focused on the role of missionaries in education and their motives.

Here I quote from the article: "While missionaries came to colonial reform through the back door, mass literacy and mass education were more deliberate projects—the consequence of a Protestant vision that knocked down old hierarchies in the name of 'the priesthood of all believers.' If all souls were equal before God, everyone would need to access the Bible in their own language. They would also need to know how to read."

So, there you have it. According to the article the missionaries' motivation to educate is that all newly converted believers can read the Bible.

Interesting, indeed, since believers in the first several centuries after the Christ had an almost identical perceived illiteracy rate as Africans did before colonialism. In truth, Africans were not illiterate before colonialism—that is a Western myth—but I am referring here to accepted statistics.

No one in those early centuries after the Christ had access to a Bible, as we know it, because it did not exist until the fourth century, and even in the fourth century, it was remarkably different from what we now call the Bible.

There is no evidence of a mass education campaign in the early church. How on earth did they survive, thrive, and grow? How did they have any concept of a "priesthood of all believers" without missionaries to educate them? In fact, considering the conversation of Jesus and Nicodemus and the Apostle Paul's statements about his own education—"I count everything as a loss in comparison to the value of knowing the Christ ..."—one would think a better argument can be made against education than for it. But even that argument is in the Bible—which did not exist, as such, in those first centuries of believers in the Christ.

So, the question becomes this. What exactly is accomplished when one culture goes and educates another culture to teach them to read and learn a book that has been translated and traditionalized through the cultural lens of the educators? Perhaps some strange and confusing ideas of God; a lily-white Jesus; bastardized concepts of the church, worship, salvation, and the meaning of the Christ?

Paul, I think, would be absolutely appalled at what the modern missionary is doing with education. May I dare say, he would call it a false gospel, as he did in Galatians when he confronted those who wanted others to conform to their culture. When he said, in his first letter to the Corinthians, "I decided to know nothing among you except Christ and Him Crucified," clearly, he was mistaken? Did he not understand that those Greek and Italian converts, who knew nothing of the Hebrew Bible, needed an education in reading Hebrew and understanding all the promises that led up to the Christ? He, it seems, was foolish enough to think that people could simply accept or reject the Christ's message and then he could simply walk away (or be carried out after a stoning)—all without an education program!

There is no precursor to Paul's message, there is no burden put on the believer other than to follow the Christ. There is no mandate on circumcision, medicine, buildings, or education. These are all Western traditionalism, and they have nothing to do with the gospel or the intended message of a believer.

Today's missionaries seem to think that they know better. They have learned to build culturally inappropriate buildings that separate young, malleable minds from parents and their parents' traditions and to inoculate these young minds (under the banner of Western enlightenment) with a good dosage of individualism, thereby keeping them from ever fully returning to their parents' world. Then the missionaries give their tutees the white Jesus and a translation of a translation through a Western lens that bears little resemblance to their own culture (which they are by then cut off from anyway). Is this what is considered an improvement on Paul's method?

If Paul had only used modern methods, he could have brought the whole world under the single banner of Hebrew culture. Oh, yes! Now I remember—Paul, in his letter to the Galatians, castigated (or at least suggested castration for) believers who behaved like this. If bringing believers under the cultural banner of Israel was considered a false gospel in Galatia, how much more of a false gospel is it to bring believers in Africa under the culture banner of the west?

Later, I intend to mention what Christ taught about the manner and message of the disciples. It is shocking to me that modern missionaries seem to ignore what their Christ has to say, but they can accept, instead, what their mission board has to say with minimal crises of conscience.

Perhaps I have pushed too far too soon. I can hear cries of "Unfair!" from both ends of the spectrum. I want to point out, however, that no matter what you think is a minimal or necessary addition to the message—be it education, medicine, famine relief, water systems— you are adding something to a message that Paul was determined to let stand on its own. Any minimal addition is the proverbial camel's nose under the tent. One simply can't add a little culture to a message without adding the entire culture. That is, in part, what the circumcision debate in the book of Acts and Galatians was all about.

Yes, I know about the many texts, such as the Sermon on the Mount, that point to the poor, needy widows, and orphans. But I dare you to find a verse that says the way to aid the least of these is to give them over to a Christian organization that will be certain to channel its funds appropriately—some of it to the needy. In fact, the entire idea of organizational help is a Western construct with devastating effects on cultures that are not so dedicated to individualism. There is a big difference between organizing ones giving to the poor (as Paul did) and giving gifts to a charitable organization.

One more swipe at the education peddled by missionaries: Why, pray tell, if the motive of the Western Protestant is Biblical literacy, do they teach everything else? Why do they teach about the finding of America, those "heroic" voyagers from Europe who discovered the New World—which apparently did not exist before they stumbled across it. It would seem their primary goal is not education; it is, instead, reeducation.

Biblical education (whatever that means) quickly becomes a sideline, useful for raising funds.

Do not protest too much. I am judging based on actions. The reality is cultures that the missionary does not understand—and often considers sinful or demonic or based in witchcraft—are met with education. Education is the antidote in the Western mind for everything of which he is ignorant. And not any education, mind you, Western education. Education, not Christ.

But can't we use Western-style education, or any education style, for that matter, to lead people to Christ? Absolutely not! If you haven't figured this out by now, please read on.

Colonialism wanted missionaries precisely because they are Western education machines. The primary reason missionaries were invited into the bosom of the colonial structure at the turn of the last century (the Golden Age of Missions) is because colonial governments and neocolonial powers knew from the previous two colonial movements exactly what happens when one sends in the missionaries. And it worked perfectly. It worked for the colonial governments and the now despot governments that followed them. And I maintain that it destroyed the message of the cross in the process.

In the National Archives in Nairobi, I found notes from colonial provincial governors outlining their monthly meetings. One report submitted at each meeting was on the progress of missionary work.

Given top billing in this report was education. The willingness of the colonial powers to grant additional areas of work to a mission society was based on that society's ability to establish schools in the areas that they were assigned. Any unwillingness on the part of a mission society to educate and the missionary endeavor would not last long in the colony. There were always plenty of other missionary societies to choose from.

Some have argued that the fact that colonial aggression and the major missionary movements happened at the same time is merely coincidental. Those who feel this way should take a journey to the archives of the countries where their favorite missionary endeavors occurred during the colonial period. They should take the time to read the level of collusion. Indeed, the ultimate motives differed between the missionaries and the colonial overlords. But the records are quite clear that the modern missionary movements and colonial expansion were anything but coincidental.

Why is it that missionaries never question the educational system they have established? Where is the literature where they have discussed more culturally appropriate methods—or where they explored teaching the gospel through the existing educational system of the cultures that they ministered to?

Better yet, where are the articles that question the basis of education as the work of missionaries at all?

The answer is simple: the educative mandate came not from God; it came, instead, from colonialism. It was easy for missionaries to justify this, as they too believed that the wretched heathen needed to be elevated to a higher level (in the earlier years that meant white man's civilization). Missionaries who were appalled at the system were removed, and the missionaries who remained became the company of the compliant. Like it or not, when it comes to education and the missionary, this is the truth.

Within a few years after encountering the colonial invasion (which is what it was), the Gikuyu people sent some of their brightest young people—among them Jomo Kenyatta—overseas to get a Western education. Their mission was to receive a Western education and bring it back to the people. The Gikuyu could see there was a lot of power in the education of the West. When these young people returned, they set up Gikuyu-run schools all over their lands. Unfortunately, they adopted some of the structure of Western education, but nevertheless, they were still self-educating within their own culture. One would think that the colonial government would have been happy and praised the natives in their enterprise and that the missionaries would have been delighted that they could return to their first directive, the gospel. But no. The government outlawed any native-run education and turned the Gikuyu schools over to—you guessed it—a missionary agency. And praise God, the relationship between the colony and the missionary grew ever stronger.

It was and is not education, per se, that matters to the colonial, neocolonial, and the missionary. It was specifically Western education that mattered/matters because it separates the student from his or her culture and ensures that they can never truly go home (or maintain continuity with their past). Not ever.

CHIEFS AND MISSIONARIES

I am going to try to do the impossible and distill volumes of information into a few short paragraphs.

The Agikuyu, like many others in East Africa, did not have a chief or chiefdom system of governance before colonialism. They had thrown off their chief system a couple hundred years before colonialism when a man, loosely translated to "King Gikuyu," ruled the Gikuyu in a tyrannical way—this king is not the same as the original Gikuyu father.

If you know anything about the historical period after the Cromwell revolution in England, perhaps you are aware of a debate that lasted almost a century subsequently. The question at hand was what, in fact, was the perfect form of government—anything but a king. Those debates resulted (for better or worse) in the American and French revolutions.

In a similar way, ruling agemates among the Gikuyu, after disposing of their tyrannical king, debated a better system of government—because they also wanted something other than a king.

What that generation of Gikuyu thinkers came up with was a combination of independent self-rule of each household, community, and clan along with a multilayered system of elder counsels who provided judicial oversight, operating at various levels throughout the culture. There was no need in their system for a legislative or executive or judicial branch. Lawsuits, disputes, and questions of procedure were brought to the appropriate elder counsel. A system of appeals was in place until, if necessary, it was brought to the ultimate elder counsel—the closest comparison would be America's Supreme Court.

Along with these levels of judicial oversight, the Gikuyu put in place a system of ritual, agemate alliances, storytelling, marriage, and teachers (gichandi), which kept the entire community together.

THE OGRE, THE HYENA, AND THE
RABBIT (OR SQUIRREL)

Among the repertoire of almost every Bantu culture is a set of similar folktales based on three characters, the ogre, the hyena, and the rabbit or squirrel. In precolonial Agikuyu folklore, the third character was a type of squirrel, but with Swahili (also a Bantu culture) becoming the lingua franca of East Africa, the Gikuyu generally adopted the Swahili use of a rabbit.

The stories that surrounded these three characters gave storytellers the basis for more than just entertainment. The three characters were designed to show the three characteristics of being human that could threaten the cohesive nature of a communal society.

The squirrel is the least harmful. This is the jokester, the one that laughs and takes delight in the well-placed prank that humiliates or embarrasses another. Most often, the laugh is played on the hyena or the ogre. But nevertheless, the one who does not take the community seriously and laughs at the expense of others can never be taken seriously. Their voice is not heard in the council of elders. They may be entertaining, but they do nothing to create unity in the culture.

The hyena is a person driven by insatiable appetite and greed, and their concern is not the cohesiveness of the people. It is always best to recognize the hyena and protect the community from their selfish ambition. They are never to be trusted, and they are never to be allowed to sit in the council of elders.

The ogre is one who appears to be a part of the culture (in our case the Gikuyu culture), but in fact, they are out to eat or devour the culture. The culture and its members are the prey. Ogres hide their features and dress and look Gikuyu. Their words are slick and enticing, and they will lead a person, a homestead, or a clan into their trap and then hold them captive as they feed on their victims.

If you are Gikuyu, you are no doubt grimacing at this cursory summary. Please forgive me. But what I want to point out is that the Agikuyu did not have chiefs, and they put in place a system of checks, songs, and stories designed to prevent the tyranny of a king or chief from ever happening again. This may surprise some of the younger members of that culture, who may have assumed that chiefs were always a part of their history.

The ogre-hyena-rabbit stories were used to insulate the Gikuyu from the types of characters that might return them to a tyrannical rule that they had disposed of for at least two centuries.

COLONIALISM

When the colonialists invaded the Gikuyu lands, they had a problem. There was no head to the Gikuyu snake for them to cut off. From the Western world's perspective, there must be a leader, even if such a one is not called a king. The Gikuyu system of cultural adhesiveness and elder judiciary made any type of top-to-bottom administration unnecessary. The Gikuyu, as well as other East African cultures, had singular figures that rose throughout their history, especially in times of crises or war, but these men were not executors, legislators, or the judiciary. They rose responding to a need and then went home to their farmlands.

But colonialism already had a solution to this problem, as it was not the first time in colonial expansion that they had encountered it. The solution: establish chiefs and negotiate only with them. This same pattern occurred in much of North America. Precolonial

Native Americans, for the most part, did not have chiefs either—at least in the Western concept of the word. Certainly, they had big men who rose to the occasion in a crisis, but chiefdom was not part of the administrative mechanism of most of their cultures.

THE MISSIONARY

How do you establish chiefs in a chief-less society, one might ask? Well, here is how it was done.

Missionaries in each "ward" were assigned as the representatives of the Gikuyu people in their area.

Imagine the audacity of this. Western born and bred, limited language skills at best, living in fortress compounds, armed with the presupposition of Western superiority, and with no background in the culture beyond a few works by Western anthropologists—how did this qualify missionaries to be the representatives of a people that became the chattel of colonialism?

The ultimate assignment or responsibility for a missionary was to find strong leaders among the Gikuyu to appoint as chiefs in the various wards.

Praise God, the missionary responds. As we win souls to Christ, we will identify those with strong leadership skills to be the chiefs of these people, and they will ultimately lead the culture to Christ.

I am going to brush past the racism and cultural bigotry of this concept. I am going to brush past the idea that missionaries were in such cahoots with the colonial scheme that they dared agree to the role given to them. I will address in some other essay, perhaps, how utterly this mission fails in the most fundamental aspects of the leadership, as defined by the Christ, that the missionary claims to follow.

Instead, I want to mention the devastation this scheme caused to the Gikuyu culture and, in my view, continues to cause today.

For the West, the marks of leadership that are most sought after are the very same marks identified in Gikuyu culture as those of the hyena and the ogre, those of a character that will destroy a people if such persons come into power. For the man who is willing to sacrifice the good of the culture for personal gain—admired in the West as a driven personality that can think outside of the cultural box—or the man who claims to be rooted in culture but entices others to leave their cultural basis destroys the culture. What the West, in its elevation of the individual over the society, finds admirable and necessary for leadership is fatal to a communal culture.

Hyenas and ogres were the easiest and first to be won to the Christianity of the missionaries. And hyenas and ogres were the men the early missionaries appointed to be among the first chiefs.

One focus of the missionary world, that is touted even to this day, is the need to raise up strong Christian leadership to help a struggling society (in this case the Agikuyu) to follow a new direction. The more missionaries think this, the more they ensure the destruction of the peoples they claim to love and serve.

The teachings about leadership in the words of the Christ are not reflected in the missionary model of leadership. On the other hand, the teachings of the Christ on leadership, and the kind of leaders to avoid, is almost identical to the Agikuyu concept of avoiding ogres and hyenas—if not also rabbits and squirrels.

I am certain that there will be howls of protest about my handling of this subject, from all sides. It will take several more sections to demonstrate my point on this matter.

When it comes to leadership, the Agikuyu had it right. The missionary world destroyed a far better understanding of leadership, in large part because they were willing accomplices of the colonial scheme.

And they are so vested in the Western concept of leadership, that they continue the carnage to this day.

Adapted from the book, *Take Nothing With You: Rethinking the Role of Missionaries*, by Skeeter Wilson, Quoir Publishing, 2020.

14

DECONSTRUCTION AND GOD'S UNCONVENTIONAL LOVE

MARK GREGORY KARRIS

"An uncontrolling God neither creates us as robots nor temporarily roboticizes us. From God's special incarnation in Jesus to activity in the smallest creatures, God acts without controlling. And this lack of control—at all levels of existence—makes loving relationships possible."
                                                          – Thomas Oord

Michael is a highly intelligent guy, passionate about God. For a long time, he would set aside a period of quiet-time when he would diligently pray and read his Bible. He would excitedly read every apologetic book he could find, was an avid evangelist passionate about defending his faith, and a faithful attendee at his church. All Michael ever talked about were the great things God was doing in his life.

He went to a church that preached what is infamously called *the prosperity gospel*. With the right amount of faith and obedience, so he was told, Michael and others could have it all: healing from sickness, financial prosperity, a family with beautiful children and a white picket fence, and confidence that God would provide them with highly successful careers (all with the right donation, of course).

Then, one day, tragedy struck. Michael's sister, who went to the same church, got into a terrible car accident and died. This tragic event would eventually lead him into the wild disorienting vortex of the deconstruction and reconstruction journey.

Like many who are on the D/R journey, Michael struggles with understanding how God could allow people to experience terrible accidents, evils, abuses, and religious traumas. This is the age-old theodicy question. Theodicy refers to the attempt by humans to make sense of how a good, loving, and omnipotent God promotes, or prevents, the harsh evils and suffering in the world.

There are others who—once the veil of Christian clichés, platitudes, puritanical doctrines, and preposterous prosperity teachings are lifted—become confused as to the true nature of God. The theodicy question is then connected to other questions like, "Where was God when I was being taught, and while I was believing, abusive and abysmal doctrines?" or "Why was God silent while I was in the midst of believing false images about who God is?" They wonder how prayer and miracles work in the midst of suffering. And, many wondered if they could ever love and trust God after being deceived, especially after believing they had an accurate depiction of who God was.

The reality of suffering, especially evil, has turned countless people away from God. It has created such enormous cognitive dissonance for folks, that some end up in a cold and distant relationship with God. I am convinced that to reconstruct our faith, we must have a theology of suffering anchored in the unconventional love of God. This is especially important in a world full of pain, suffering, confusion, sorrow, and death. I believe that the unconventional love of God is shown in God's perfect, moment-to-moment, uncontrolling, and co-operative love.

MY CLOUDY OFFERING

I hesitate to offer a theology of suffering and an overall theodicy that can help us make sense of the nature, or working, of God in the world. I do it out of reverence, knowing I am walking on sacred, blood-stained ground. Treading carefully, I am trying to make sense of where and how God fits in with real people's everyday trauma, abuses of various kinds, social injustices, and the unspeakable evil that surrounds us all. I don't take these situations lightly.

People who advocate for an anti-theodicy position resonate with me. I mean, humans trying to understand God are like an intelligent monkey trying to understand the mechanics of spaceflight. There is an absurdity to anyone saying, "Let me give you a God's-eye view of who God is and exactly how God works in the world." In offering a theodicy as it relates to deconstruction, I am also mindful that I don't want to fully take God off the hook. I don't want to absolve God of all of the brutality of human existence or the tragic fate of all other forms of life. I don't want to rob people of the natural experiences and expressions of lament and protest in the face of such appalling realities.

Yet, as I shared earlier, when talking about God, I must give it a shot. The risk of giving the main stage to theodicies that are based on a controlling, all-powerful, autocratic, and authoritarian God is too great. The countless victims of *God is in control of everything* theodicies are too much to bear. I cannot sit idly by while mumbling, "Well, it *is* a mystery. Who can really know?"

I can relate to that great mystic, the apostle Paul, who wrote: "Ever since the creation of the world his eternal power and divine nature, invisible though they are, have been understood and seen through the things he has made" (Romans 1:20, NRSV). He's right. We can understand aspects of God's nature by reflecting on our experiences of creation and life itself. All of the complexity, richness, diversity, beauty, and grotesqueness of life says something about God. We are not in *total* darkness. But we "see only a reflection as in a mirror" and "know in part" (1 Cor. 13:12) when it comes to truth in general. I admit, when it comes to understanding the mysteries of free will, suffering, and God's sovereignty, the mirror is a bit foggier than normal, making it difficult to flesh out a perfectly accurate reflection.

Despite the difficulties of seeing perfectly and clearly, I am compelled to share my imperfect monkey truth. Being that this is only a chapter, I assure you it will bring up more questions than answers. However, I offer it in the hopes that it removes a few unnecessary obstacles to your relationship with the Divine. My desire for this chapter is to help you reconstruct an image of God that is saturated in God's love, without making you leave your brain at the door.

The remainder of this chapter will briefly explore God's perfect, moment-to-moment, uncontrolling, and co-operative love through the lens of constructive theology, philosophy, the biblical witness, and my experience. Also included is a brief examination of what God's love means for important topics that come up on the journey of deconstruction, such as our soul wear, evil, petitionary prayer and justice, trust, and miracles.[84]

---

84. For a more extensive overview of these topics, I encourage you to read my book, *Divine Echoes* and Thomas Oord's book, *God Can't.*

GOD'S PERFECT, MOMENT-TO-MOMENT LOVE

In the book of Matthew, Jesus says to his disciples "Be perfect, therefore, as your heavenly Father is perfect."[85]

Okay. If we are to be perfect like God, we must ask ourselves in what way is God perfect?

Some think that perfection is all about not sinning. "Stop being so worldly, Christian! Be perfect as God is perfect!" shouts the angry preacher.

Jesus' plea for perfection has caused some Christians to feel an enormous amount of guilt and shame. They feel they have to be perfect and never sin. If they do sin, they think God will be furious at them. However, the context of the verse reveals that perfection has nothing to do with sin management. Rather, it has everything to do with how we are called to love others. The invitation is to *love* as God perfectly *loves*.

So, how does God perfectly love? Let's look at the immediate context. God "causes his sun to rise on the evil and the good, and sends rain on the righteous and the unrighteous" (Matthew 5:45b). Did you catch that? We are called to emulate God's perfect, unconditional, all-inclusive love—even with people on our naughty list. This is why Jesus says in the previous verse, "Love your enemies and pray for those who persecute you, that you may be children of your Father in heaven" (Matthew 5:44–45). In telling his listeners to love their enemies, Jesus is asking them to love like God does. How does one do that? Recognizing that God demonstrates perfect prodigal love by loving those who do not love God back: prayer-less, disobedient, and God-ignoring enemies.

We do not wish, pray, or beg God's nature into existence. God is perfect love. God loves. That is who God is and what God does. God's perfect love extends to all. The birds do not pray, but a loving God takes care of them (Matthew 6:26). The lilies do not intercede, yet God is mindful of them (Matthew 6:28). Enemies and persecutors of God's children do not pray, but God loves them (Matthew

85. Matthew 5:48

5:43–48; Luke 6:27). The ungrateful and wicked do not pray, yet God is kind to them (Luke 6:35). God "so loved the world" without the prompting of prayer (John 3:16). God exists as who God is: a God of love. God's attributes—God's holiness, justice, mercy, and power—are funneled through that love.

God's love is perfect and active. Moment-to-moment, in every creature's life, God seeks to maximize goodness, beauty, truth, love, and healing while minimizing evil. God never sits on the bench, or on the sidelines, excitedly waiting to be called upon to venture into the game of life. God is not casually hanging out, sitting on his blinged-out chair made by the purest and most reverent of carpenter angels. God isn't good some of the time; God is good all the time. Right now, in this very moment, God is up to something. In each moment, we can become grace catchers, those who are aware of what Divine love is up to and enter into that grace-filled love adventure.

GOD'S UNCONTROLLING AND CO-OPERATIVE LOVE

There are things God cannot do. God cannot lie (Hebrews 6:18); God cannot be tempted (James 1:13); God cannot be prejudiced (Acts 10:34–35); God cannot sin (Deuteronomy 32:4); and God cannot get tired (Isaiah 40:28). Due to the nature of God's uncontrolling love, it is not that God can control creatures and chooses not to do so, but perhaps God cannot control creatures due to God's very loving nature. Simply put, love does not control. Therefore, God does not singlehandedly control others. That's why we call it *uncontrolling love.*[86]

God is doing all God can do to maximize good and to minimize evil, but God is constrained by God's love. Love must preserve the

---

86. For a deeper understanding of the topic of God's uncontrolling love, see Oord, Thomas J. *The Uncontrolling Love of God: An Open and Relational Account of Providence.* Downers Grove, IL: InterVarsity Press, 2016.

sanctity of free will even at the cost of what people with free will choose. To disregard and usurp free will is to cease being loving.

Suggesting God *cannot* unilaterally control people or events, and manipulate them as God sees fit, is of huge theological significance. Many Christians do not hold to this idea because it implies God is not all powerful. For some, the idea that God is not all powerful, implies that God is weak. For example, the Christian philosopher, William Hasker, describes one common perspective: "God's capacity to control the detailed course of events is limited only by his self-restraint, not by any inability to do so."[87] He reiterates what I said before: many Christians believe God can control but chooses not to. It is a complete paradigm shift (a heretical shift for some) to suggest that God simply *cannot* control because of God's uncontrolling, loving nature.

Just because God does not *unilateral* control, however, does not mean God is unable to exercise any kind of control at all. God is not passive and powerless. God's control is a different kind of control. God's power is a different kind of power. According to the Oxford dictionary, the word *control* can mean "the power to influence or direct people's behavior or the course of events."[88] I suggest God lovingly and powerfully influences us by inviting, empowering, inspiring, filling, convicting, leading, comforting, healing, and challenging us toward ever-increasing experiences of shalom. And God does this without coercion or force.

It is not enough to say that God's love is uncontrolling. It's a negative statement about what God *can't* do (God can't control others). We need to also talk positively about what God's love *can* do. God's love is *co-operative*, meaning God requires mutual assistance and collaboration to accomplish God's goals. An idea that Thomas Oord so eloquently reminds us in his book, *The Uncontrolling Love of God*, is that God never intervenes in the world unilaterally; God

87. William Hasker, *God, Time, and Knowledge* (Ithaca, NY: Cornell University Press, 1989), 196, author's italics removed.

88. "Control," *Oxford Dictionary of English, 3rd ed.* (Oxford: Oxford University Press, 2010).

never acts alone, of God's own accord, disregarding lawlike regularities (a.k.a. the laws of nature) and the free will of people. On the contrary, God always works through willing cooperation.

Let's explore what the unconventional love of God—God's perfect, moment-to-moment, uncontrolling, and co-operative love—looks like in our everyday lives, especially as it relates to our D/R journey.

GOD'S UNCONVENTIONAL LOVE AND SOUL WEAR

God's silence in the midst of my yearning for truth has pained me more times than I can remember. I can recall countless times, humbly lying in my bed with tears in my eyes, crying to God, begging God to reveal God's self to me.

"Why, God, are you silent?! I just want the truth! I am confused. I don't know what to believe. Just tell me what the hell I should believe, and I will believe it! Please, I beg you, speak to me."

I was desperate to hear God's voice. I wanted God to set the record straight. The God who created the universe should surely be able to talk to me as if I was talking to a friend. Right? Sadly, the crickets amidst the silence of God's voice was deafening. The existential aloneness in those eternal moments filled me with crushing agony.

How did we get thrown into the deconstruction and reconstruction journey and become so disoriented? How did people's soul wear, and people's soul wear before them, get God so wrong? Why did our soul wear and our internal beliefs of God become so distorted? Why didn't God simply stop people from teaching and believing heresy? Why does God continue to allow us to be in a constant state of confusion?

The Unfolding Process

God, whose love is uncontrolling, is not forcefully in control of history. So, keeping God's unconventional love in mind, it makes sense that human beings are in an ever-unfolding process of physical, spiritual, and emotional growth. God is moment-to-moment and non-coercively luring creatures toward the Divine aim of evolving experiences of love, goodness, beauty, and truth. God's co-operative love invites simple and complex organisms to cooperate and to dance together toward evolving organismic artistry.

It is hard to believe that we went from wiggly, single-cell organisms to sentient human beings over billions of years. And it is wild to imagine that we were once sacredly drawing on cave walls, looking up at the moon in deferential awe as if it were a god. Now we are drawing on advanced computer systems and have stepped onto the moon, symbolically declaring that we are gods. All of life is in process, including our image of God.

It is very apparent, with thousands of different religions out there—and over 30,000 different Christian sects and denominations—that humans are a creative and diverse bunch. We love to create and imagine and then arrogantly think our creative imaginations are *the* truth.

What is also apparent is that God doesn't have a pattern of materializing into human form to declaratively and definitively tell us who is right and who is wrong. Referring to God's inspiration in our lives and those of the biblical writers, pastor and theologian Gregory Boyd writes, "God refuses to undermine the personhood and freedom of people by lobotomizing them so that they perfectly conform to his will…God respects the integrity of a mutually impacting relationship, which is what a relationship of love requires."[89]

Our views of goodness, beauty, and truth—including our image of who God is—cannot be forcefully manipulated to correspond completely to God's truth. The truth God is trying to convey to us can't be instantly and coercively downloaded. Even being in love with Jesus doesn't completely solve the issue of perfect knowledge.

89. Gregory A. Boyd, *Crucifixion of the Warrior God: Volumes 1 & 2* (Minneapolis: Augsburg Fortress, 2017), 491–92.

I could say that Christ is the definitive revelation of God and that he solves all the answers to our questions of who God is. The problem is that there is no Christian consensus on the exact details of who God is through Jesus, what Jesus came to do, and what Jesus meant when he sought to describe the life to come.

While the Spirit is in all, while all creatures manifest and reveal the Spirit, and as Jesus reveals God in an unmatched fullness, God is continually revealing deeper levels of revelation of God's wonder, beauty, truth, and nature as if through faint radio waves. We are constantly tuning into the frequency of the Divine, never arriving at a destination, but always learning and evolving (and sometimes, devolving). The problem is that we like to think we have arrived. We are terrifically creative, tragically tribal, and commonly prone to thinking we have all the right answers.

Case in point: I find it utterly fascinating that whether people are Calvinist, Arminian, Essential Kenosist, Universalist, Hopeful Universalist, Process Theologian, PSA Enthusiast, Proponent for a Non-Violent God, Premillennial, Amillennial, Cessationist, Inerrantist, Exclusivist, Inclusivist, Creationist, Dispensationalist, Covenantalist, or Open Theist, rarely do they admit to obvious contradictions in their position. No one ever says, "I've read all 31,000 biblical verses and there are some that contradict my position." They say the exact opposite and engage in incredible hermeneutical gymnastics to prove the flawlessness of their biblically superior theological position.

Not only does the above phenomenon show the incredibly creative mental feats involved in maintaining a homogenous theological position, it also demonstrates the epitome of cognitive bias and pride. It also shows us that God, whose love is uncontrolling, lets non-coercive love take its course alongside the imaginations of humankind. Since God, as a spirit, doesn't have vocal cords, God cannot shout loud enough for people to hear what is absolutely true. So, theologies continue to multiply—with no end in sight.

Trust the God in You

It can be scary for those of us on the D/R journey to trust God again. I get it. How could we jump in with both feet after we've been burned before by false theologies? The best encouragement I can give you is an invitation to sit at the feet of Christ, who is love. Sit in silence. Embrace mystery. Allow the mystery that is Love, to guide you into all truth. Then, do the unthinkable. As you are in community with God and others, trust in your experience. I know that *experience* gets such a bad rap. But, unfortunately, the alternative is to trust everyone else's experience and how *they* inter-pret the scriptures, God, and reality. My hope for you is that, just like the Apostle Paul did, you will allow God's perfect, moment-to-moment, uncontrolling, and co-operative love to lead you into truth.

Paul's Example

It is incredible that Paul wrote about 50,000 words, or 28%, of the New Testament (more or less, depending on which books you believe he authored). Do you know what percentage of those words Paul explicitly used to quote Jesus' sayings from the gospels? Probably 2% or less. That's right. Not much! What does that mean? I am sure it could mean many things, but for me, it points to the liberating invitation to be who we are in God and to value our own experiences. That's exactly what the Apostle Paul did!

Paul was obviously familiar with the oral tradition, and the incredible stories passed down to him, concerning Jesus. He was an exquisite teacher of the law and knew the Hebrew scriptures very well (he quoted about 100 of them in the NT). Most impor-tantly, Paul was also head over heels in love with Christ. He was completely Christ-centered. All things were rubbish, he said, apart from Christ.

Still, rather than memorizing and quoting what others said about Jesus, or what others said Jesus said, Paul spoke from his own experience. It seemed, that out of the deep, intimate relationship he had with Jesus, Paul spoke his truth. And his truth, as he marinated himself in the presence of God, now constitutes much of the New Testament.

Paul did not just settle for others' experiences of Jesus. He did not feel the need to quote Jesus secondhand to share powerful and provocative spiritual truths. He did not say, "Well, since I can't find what I am saying explicitly in the scriptures, or verbatim from Jesus' words as quoted by others, it must not be worthy of sharing. Out of his profound mystical relationship with Jesus, he began to connect the dots between love and law—between his newly found captivation with Jesus and the religious-saturated Hebraic world he thought he knew and understood.

Paul lived in Christ, through Christ, with Christ, and for Christ. He was bold and courageous enough to be congruent with how Jesus was leading and guiding him. He took creative risks and liberties, despite the nay-saying of religious heresy hunters, to convey how he understood the world around him and the sacred Hebrew Scriptures. And, don't miss this: he also did it in community with other people struck by the fierce arrow of Jesus' love.

I encourage you to be free, to live and speak out of that intimate place you have with Christ. Be courageous to share what God has placed in your heart and mind. You are not less spiritual if you don't quote five of Jesus' sayings before and after you share your truth. Share and wrestle in community (including the community of saints and sinners found in the Hebrew Bible and New Testament), so that their divinely inspired truths can either validate your experience, expand your vision, or temper it. Sometimes, you may even need to be a pyro-theological trendsetter, setting ablaze what has come before you. Other times, in humility, you may have to admit you went too far.

Will your truth be perfect? Definitely not. Whose is? Will your truth be revised? I am sure it will change over time. Sarah Bessey writes,

> *The more I tried to keep God contained, the more God insisted on escaping from my fetters. Every time I build a box for God, God transcended that box...while still somehow often abiding within it to meet me there. Every time I think I have it figured out—this is how*

God acts, this is who God is, this is what God will do, this is what God expects—that reorienting, bracing, dangerous Love becomes and unbecomes again. And so I have been made and remade and unmade over and over again in response to the ancient one.[90]

All of us are in process. Sometimes we get it right, sometimes we get it wrong, but oftentimes it is a mix of both. All of us will have theological truths that are likened to wood, hay, and straw that will eventually be burned in the refining fire of God's love. But we need to accept that this is where we are now. If we wait until our truths are viewed perfectly through shiny and transparent glass that peers into the heavenlies, then we will be waiting for quite some time. Until then, you have permission to be congruent, to be authentic, and to share *your* embodied truth, through *your* unique soul wear, with the world!

GOD'S UNCONVENTIONAL LOVE, EVIL, AND SUFFERING

No doubt the theodicy question, in relation to evil and suffering, is one of the most perplexing questions to wrestle with. It is also one of the main reasons people either ditch God, stay distant roommates with God, or never want to introduce themselves to God in the first place. Well-known author and pastor Timothy Keller writes, "As I took up life as a minister, I tried to understand why so many people resisted and rejected God. I soon realized that perhaps the main reason was affliction and suffering."[91]

Evil, loss, and suffering are common to all people, in all places, regions, and socioeconomic statuses. No one can escape the effects of suffering, no matter how rich or poor they are, or where they live on earth. The truth is that if you don't have an adequate understanding, the weight of evil, loss, and suffering can crush you. Your

90. Sarah Bessey, *Miracles and Other Reasonable Things: A Story of Unlearning and Relearning God.* (New York: Howard Books, Atria, 2019).

91. Timothy Keller, *Walking with God through Pain and Suffering* (New York: Penguin Books, 2016), 4.

theology can either deepen your suffering or bring deep consolation during your D/R journey.

When people think about the concept of evil, they typically think of heinous and morally reprehensible acts like murder, rape, and genocide. While all of these acts are evil, the biblical concept of evil is much broader. Simply put, evil is anything contrary to the will of God, such as thoughts (Gen. 6:5), deeds (Prov. 5:22), desires (Rom. 6:12), spirits (Mark 3:11), etc.

Thomas Oord writes about useless pain and suffering, calling it *genuine evil*. Oord writes, "Genuine evil events cause more harm than the good that could have occurred."[92] A child being sexually assaulted is a genuine evil. A pastor stealing money from his congregants is a genuine evil. A person commanding genocide is a genuine evil. Suffering is an inner, cognitive/emotional reaction to these kinds of experiences.

Where there is evil, suffering is usually not far behind; however, where there is suffering, evil is not always present. For example, a child who is told by his parents to go to bed early may experience suffering while the event of going to bed early is not necessarily an evil act.

So, what does God's perfect, moment-to-moment, uncontrolling, and co-operative love have to do with the conundrum of the reality of evil? Everything!

Thomas Oord, probably the most articulate theologian championing God's uncontrolling love, writes: "To be transformed, we must reform our beliefs. . . reconstructing requires changing our view of God's power. We should not blame God for evil because God cannot prevent it singlehandedly. God neither causes nor allows suffering but always expresses uncontrolling love."[93]

Due to God's love, God doesn't force God's way into people's lives; that would be contradictory to God's nature. So, evil exists, to

92. Thomas Jay Oord, God Can't: How to Believe in God and Love after Tragedy, Abuse, or Other Evils (SacraSage Press, 2019), 14.

93. Oord, 87.

the extent that it does, because a loving and uncontrolling God, by God's very nature, cannot forcefully stop people from choosing to commit evil acts.

Think about the alternative. Do we really want to believe that God has the power to singlehandedly stop evil from occurring, but simply chooses not to?

What would we think of a man, watching a child be sexually assaulted, having the power to stop the event from happening, but simply choosing not to help? Our inner spirit captivated by love and justice would passionately rise up and object to the unjust and immoral actions of that man. In the same way, our spirit would also rise up against a view of God as someone with full ability to intervene in horrific events, but who simply chooses not to help (but unfairly decides to help others).

As much as we yearn for God to unilaterally control people and forcefully stop individuals from committing acts of evil, like *The Dark Phoenix* of the Marvel Universe, God simply cannot. We wish God, on occasion, would ignore free will and knock a rapist unconscious before he engages in a violent transgression, but it is simply outside the bounds of what God can do. God can't stop evil like a divine Whack-A-Mole. God also can't disregard lawlike regularities and stop a tsunami from killing hundreds of thousands of innocent people.

Those who are angry at God, because of the world we live in, want an altogether different world than the one we have. When asked what the world would look like if a loving, uncontrolling, and non-coercive God actually exists, people struggle to articulate another possibility. Given that love takes risks and doesn't force, coerce, control, or manipulate, how would that kind of God work in this world? It seems that if we took God's unconventional love seriously, we would end up with precisely the world we find ourselves in—a world where free creatures, randomness, and lawlike regularities can run amok, sometimes in the direction of beauty, other times in the direction of destruction.

GOD'S UNCONVENTIONAL LOVE, PRAYER, AND JUSTICE

Amidst all of the topics of deconstruction, the effectiveness and coherency of petitionary prayer, especially to battle rampant evil and injustice, or to bring solace and healing to hurting and sick people, is definitely on the top of many people's lists. I will only scratch the surface of the conversation here.

Once the fantasy of a controlling God, and an "everything happens for a reason" philosophy goes out the window, people start wondering about petitionary prayer. They may ask questions, such as:

- Does prayer work?
- What exactly happens after the words leave our lips or after we speak them silently? Does God instantly hear them? Or do they first move through the traffic of heaven where angels and demons are engaged in an epic battle?
- Does a person who prays for God to heal their ill father give God extra power, energy, or motivation to do so?
- Is persistent petitionary prayer performed simply to annoy God, so that God will eventually, although begrudgingly, do the right thing and answer those prayers, as in the parable of the persistent widow and uncaring judge (Luke 18:1–18)?
- Is more prayer better? Does God increase his active love because a larger number of people pray? Does God say, "Well, just twenty of you prayed. If thirty of you had prayed, I would definitely have healed him"?
- If an all-powerful God could single-handedly save and deliver loved ones, but allows them to get into fatal accidents, become sick, be raped, or experience other tragedies because people did not pray for them, is that consistent with what a loving God would do?
- Does petitionary prayer only change us—the ones who are praying—or does it change God in some way?

Petitionary prayers are requests to God for answers to life's questions and concerns. They are also pleas for God to be the sole responsible agent to act on behalf of the one who is praying. I define the traditional understanding of the typical petitionary prayer as *talking to God and asking God to love in a specific manner in which God was not doing so beforehand.* Here is the bottom line: the perfect, moment-to-moment, uncontrolling, and co-operative love of God drastically changes the ballgame of the intersection between petitionary prayer and issues of justice and moral responsibility. Our petitionary prayers can either increase the severity of injustice or they can increase the level of shalom. Let me explain.

- Every 10 seconds, a child dies from hunger.
- Every 98 seconds another American is sexually assaulted
- Every 33.5 minutes, someone is murdered.
- Over 52,000 will die from drug overdoses this year
- On a single night in January 2015, 564,708 people experienced homelessness.

For me, if the traditional understanding of petitionary prayer doesn't work as we suppose, then these statistics are evidence that the stakes are *too high to ignore.* If we believe that by simply talking to God (or begging God), that God can singlehandedly force God's will to occur in situations and in people's lives, then we are engaging in an immature form of petitionary prayer, and ultimately, a superstitious practice. We cannot engage in spiritual activities that cause us to feel good, thinking we are accomplishing great things, but ultimately not achieving the good we set out to accomplish, or worse: contributing to the evil and suffering in the world.

The Bystander Effect

"The bystander effect" is a term used by social psychologists to describe what happens when individuals fail to intervene during crises or emergencies when they perceive others are present and aware of the event. Preeminent social psychologist Elliot Aronson writes in his classic book, *The Social Animal,* "If people are aware that an event is being witnessed by others, the responsibility felt by any individual is diffused".[94]

---

94. Elliot Aronson, *The Social Animal.* 11th ed. (New York: Worth Publishers, 2012), 51.

I became familiar with the term after reading A. M. Rosenthal's, *Thirty-Eight Witnesses: The Kitty Genovese Case.* The book is an account of the brutal rape and murder of Kitty Genovese, which occurred on March 13, 1964. It was reported there were thirty-eight people who were aware that the horrific event was occurring but did nothing to stop it. In a more recent occurrence in 2009, Dominik Brunner was murdered by two 18-year-olds. Dominik was trying to stop the violent teens from attacking other children. Unfortunately, his sacrificial gesture led to his death. Like the Genovese case, people witnessed Brunner being attacked, but no one adequately intervened to stop it.

Of course, all is not so grim for humanity. There are plenty of stories demonstrating heroic acts by bystanders. The research shows the bystander effect lessens when there are perceived real emergencies, when perpetrators are present, and when physical harm is imminent.[95] Nonetheless, the bystander effect is a genuine social phenomenon.

Have you ever witnessed violence, unethical practices, a crime, a beating, theft, bullying, or other harmful acts and done nothing about it? Sadly, I know I have.

Why am I talking about the bystander effect?

It has been my contention that the traditional practice of petitionary prayer contributes to further evil and suffering in the world. I know; it is quite the claim. I suggest the bystander effect may be one dynamic among many behind this problem.

If people believe an all-powerful and controlling God is aware of the person or situation being prayed for, then it is easy for them to become passive bystanders. When praying, it is easy to believe, "Well, God is powerful. God has a plan. God is in control. And God is going to take care of it." Unfortunately, that is exactly the kind of thinking some bystanders have when horrific violence is

95. Fischer, P., J. I. Krueger, T. Greitemeyer, C. Vogrincic, A. Kastenmüller, D. Frey, and M. Kainbacher. "The bystander-effect: A meta-analytic review on bystander intervention in dangerous and non-dangerous emergencies." *Psychological Bulletin* 137, no. 4 (2011): 517–37. doi:10.1037/a0023304.

occurring: "Well, there are plenty of people watching. Surely, there are more competent people than me who are going to take care of it. I am sure someone has called 911 by now."

When someone engages in the typical petitionary prayer, God becomes the competent, grand Witness who diffuses human responsibility; the bystander effect is on full display. The problem is the bystander effect can have terrible consequences. Suffering increases exponentially. Death can be a result. If I believe the most loving and powerful divine agent is on the scene, then there is a natural easing of the direness of the situation. If God is taking care of it, then perhaps I don't have to. I can lift my prayers up and then go about business as usual.

Let's say there are immigrant children who are taken from their parents and forced to be confined in subpar conditions to anxiously be with people they do not know. They are suffering physically, emotionally, and spiritually. After hearing about this heartbreaking news, a well-meaning church comes together and prays:

- "God, pour out your love on those children."
- "God, comfort those children."
- "God, bring justice swiftly."
- "God, I bind the enemy in Jesus's name."
- "God, change the leaders' hearts."
- "God, change the policies that are in place so this does not continue to happen."

The prayers above are coming from sincere hearts. But, in this case, sincerity without action can perpetuate further harm and suffering. You see, we already know God's stance on the issue. God hates when children are mistreated (just read Luke 17:1–4). It is not God's will for children to suffer such anguish. God already loves the children. God is already seeking to comfort the children to the extent they are able to receive God's comfort. God already desires to bring swift justice. God already wants the enemy to be bound. God already wants policies changed. God already wants leaders' hearts changed. God's love transcends ours. If we want the wellbeing of those children, don't you think God wants it exponentially more?

The problem is God cannot singlehandedly bring all of this about. Due to God's uncontrolling love, God is constrained from forcefully changing hearts, manipulating people's wills, and coercing people to change policies. God is not a puppeteer. Don't you think that if God could instantly change the outcome, God would? Does God really need to be begged to do what God does best, which is to love? What kind of God has the power to do something about those innocent, suffering children, but simply chooses not to?

It is one thing if our primary goal is sharing our heart and desires passionately with God. That is a beautiful and intimate endeavor. It is another to believe those energetic prayers somehow equip, move, inspire, or empower God to single-handedly change a person or circumstance. If people believe that praying to God in a certain manner, at a certain volume, and with certain words will convince God to single-handedly root out prejudice, abolish dehumanizing policies, reduce hate crimes, solve the problem of homelessness, heal drug addicts, stop people from committing arson, stop rapes from occurring, and so on, they are engaging in magical thinking and superstition of the worst kind.

Petitionary prayers can become an ironic gesture. Their intent may be to increase God's loving activity and shalom in the world. But prayer becomes problematic when we unknowingly and inadvertently pass the responsibility of shalom solely to God ("God, *you* fix the problem!"). We thereby avoid God's primary method through which God achieves shalom: humans, filled and led by the Spirit of God, fulfilling their vocation as God's empowered emissaries.

Praying for the Homeless

In New York City, a congregation gathered for a prayer meeting. A winter storm was expected the following day, so they took time to pray for a group of homeless people who frequented an area not too far from the church: "God, pour out your love on the homeless people downtown. Help them find shelter. Protect them from the cold and from illness. Show them the salvation of your dear Son, Jesus Christ."

Perhaps those church members were the ones who needed to be saved from the pitfalls of petitionary prayer. They may have meant well, but their prayers stemmed from a belief that talking to God (which is what prayer is) would absolve them of any responsibility to do something about the problem and, instead, placed all responsibility upon God. Ironically, instead of being beneficial, their prayers got in the way of God being able to use that congregation as his Spirit-led and empowered emissaries to love, help, and save those homeless people. God is not the one who needs to be coaxed, persuaded, or reminded in any way to love the homeless. God longs for them to be holistically saved and grieves that some will suffer in the freezing cold. If prayer in its simplest form is an act of talking, then perhaps God whispered to that congregation: "Church, pour out your love on the homeless people downtown. Help them to find shelter. Protect them from the cold and from illness. Show them the salvation of my dear Son, Jesus."

Conspiring Prayer

Keeping in mind God's perfect, moment-to-moment, uncontrolling, and cooperative love, I have proposed and detailed a model of petitionary prayer, in my book *Divine Echoes,* called "conspiring prayer." In today's world, the word "conspire" has a negative connotation: to plot with someone to do something wrong or evil. However, the English word *conspire* comes from the Latin word *conspirare*, which literally means "to breathe together" and "to act in harmony toward a common end." I combine both definitions to express what I mean by conspiring prayer.

Conspiring prayer is performed *with* God rather than *to* God. Conspiring prayer is a form of prayer where we create space in our busy lives to align our hearts with God's heart, where our spirit and God's Spirit breathe harmoniously together, and where we plot together to subversively overcome evil with acts of love and goodness (Romans 12:21). This subversive sacred practice calls forth thankful, open-hearted listeners who humbly petition and partner with God to become divine echoes, committed to bringing forth shalom in the world.

God always seeks to lovingly decrease the injustice in the world and meet the basic needs of humanity and the rest of his creation. Basic needs are needs for God to love, heal, save, and deliver from the most fundamental obstacles in the way human flourishing. For example, a basic need is to be free from poverty. God never desires that people, deprived of sustenance, starve to death. Another basic need is to be free from racism and oppression. It is never God's will for people to suffer discrimination because of the way they look, their gender, or because of their race (and so on). Other basic needs include a world without violence and genocide and a world in which healing from devastating injuries and accidents can occur. A basic spiritual need is one of salvation. God always desires people to be saved and to know his love intimately.

God's primary medium for providing basic needs is through people. God has an open-door policy. God continually looks for open-hearted faith on the earth and seeks the cooperation of human beings to co-steward creation toward shalom. While the motivation to pray common, petitionary prayers for the basic needs of others is derived from a pure inner spirit, we need to recognize that God is already actively seeking to meet those needs. God isn't keeping us from shalom, but *we* are.

If we are caught in flooding from a dangerous hurricane, and are about to drown in a car, do we really want to rely on some saints' "thoughts and prayers?" Or, do we want to rely on thoughtful and prayerful people who take courageous action? I am sure you would desire the latter. The same goes for how we respond to the basic needs of others and issues of social justice. God always loves us and is willing to provide for our needs. Moment to moment, God also offers pathways for us to share with those in need. We can prayerfully join in on what God is doing or we can choose not to.

GOD'S UNCONVENTIONAL LOVE AND MIRACLES

I can't tell you how many times I've heard, "I can't hold to your view of God's perfect, moment-to-moment, uncontrolling, and co-operative love because I believe in miracles." There is abso-lutely nothing inherent in a view of God's unconventional love that implies a belief that God can't perform miracles.

I do believe in miracles, but I do so without believing God single-handedly and forcefully intervenes to bring them about. Certainly, I can affirm that breathing, sunrises, and the body's ability to heal itself are miracles, but the more mysterious miracles that jolt the senses, and wow our hearts and minds, can also occur.

God is never coercive and is always working toward greater expe-riences of shalom on the earth. So, I have to imagine that miracles are synergistic encounters between God and cooperative agencies, cells, elements, quarks, and many other variables. Imagine a per-son who has cancer and experiences the "miracle" of healing. When God's loving power + a faith-filled and humble heart + cooperative cells and organs of a body + the right temperature + loving and compassionate others + the right nutrients + a myriad of other vari-ables come together, it could = a healing miracle.

Yes, miracles can happen. However, since God cannot coerce or control others or situations, God requires cooperation for miracles to occur. Thomas Oord, in his book *The Uncontrolling Love of God*, writes: "God's self-giving love invites creaturely cooperation for radically surprising actions that promote overall well-being. For this reason, miracles are neither coercive interventions nor the result of natural causes alone. Miracles occur when creatures, organisms, or entities of various size and complexity cooperate with God's initiat-ing and empowering love."[96]

I can't imagine the lack of miracles we see around us has any-thing to do with God's willingness. That is what the alternative view suggests. In the alternative, traditional view of miracles, God picks and chooses who to heal and who not to heal. God can do what God wants to do, when God wants to do it, and how God wants to do it. God can perform miracles apart from any coopera-tion from humans, cells, and laws of regularity. Apparently, within

96. Oord, 200.

this understanding, God appears much of the time *not* to want to perform miracles and heal those who are suffering, to stop people from raping and killing others, or to prevent kids from brutally suffering and suddenly dying from cancer.

In my understanding of miracles, because God's nature is love—and love doesn't force, coerce, or unilaterally control—God cannot always heal. One view says God *can* but chooses *not* to heal. Another says God *wants* to heal, but simply *can't*.

The view of God's uncontrolling love and a "God Can't" approach is not in contradiction with "God Can." When we say, "God Can't," we are just saying "God can't perform miracles singlehandedly without any cooperation from people, laws of regularity, and other dynamics." When folks say, "I can't get on board with the 'God Can't' model because I have seen weird stuff or miracles happen," I get confused as to why they imagine the two ideas are mutually exclusive?

Those who hold to a view of an uncontrolling, loving God would never say God can't perform miracles in people's lives. They would say it is not the case that God intentionally chooses to heal some and not others. Rather, miracles happen when God and other variables synergistically align and work together with one another. Because of that, some get healed while many others do not.

So, where does the mystery really lie? Does the mystery have to lie with whether or not God can heal but chooses not to? Is that who God is? The kind of God who has the power to instantly heal anyone, but unfairly heals some while allowing others to suffer? Does God say, "I will instantly heal five-year old Suzy from leukemia, but I will not heal five-year old Maria with leukemia?" Isn't it more plausible that God doesn't singlehandedly and coercively heal people? Perhaps it is better to suggest that "The mystery does not lie in whether God can but chooses not to; instead it lies in not knowing what variables came together and cooperated with God to cause this miracle to occur."

A view of God's uncontrolling love, in the context of a world in which miracles and healings do not happen, provides a compassionate framework for Christians. There are, I believe, too many

Christians who are bogged down by the weight of shame because they look at others who are healed and ask, "Why not me?" They conclude something is wrong with their faith, their prayer life, or themselves. Lack of healing should never be blamed on a lack of faith; that would be cruel. It's important to understand that God is in relationship with more than just human agency. There are other doors that need to be open for God to accomplish creative, relational endeavors, such as miracles.

GOD'S UNCONVENTIONAL LOVE AND TRUSTING GOD

Everyone has heard the phrase "trust in God!" It is a powerful phrase that is often used by people who suppose God is in control of all things. In some circles, it encourages listeners to surrender to an all-powerful God who—it's implied—can snap Divine fingers and instantly give them their heart's desires, making their circumstances right again. I question the accuracy of that view. Keeping in mind God's perfect, moment-to-moment, uncontrolling, and cooperative love, is there another way to understand "trust in God"? I think there is.

If we are encouraged to "trust in God," a good question to ask is: "What can we trust God for?" If we trust in God, does that mean we will never get into a terrible accident and lose both of our legs? Does that phrase mean we will never die in a horrific bombing? Does that phrase mean we will never be betrayed by a good friend or by an unfaithful partner? Does it mean we can trust that our children would not be harmed, murdered, get cancer, or die a painful death?

I know mine is not the most uplifting and traditionally pastoral sentiment, but I have come to the stark realization that I can't trust God to single-handedly stop any of the above events from happening. I don't think anyone can. Truth is, bad things can happen to anyone, at any moment. No one is promised their next second of life. No one is promised a life free from harm. Why? Bad stuff happens in this world, including vicious evil, precisely because God is not in control of all things. What else would we expect in a world where love and freedom are at the core of reality?

Today, we are bombarded with horrific stories and shocking images all day long. And this overwhelming evidence of evil creates an enormous amount of cognitive dissonance that demands a verdict. The idea of a Blueprint God, sovereignly in control of all things like a Grand Puppet Master, is untenable. Anyone who claims that God is in control of all things is implicitly stating that God is the Grand purveyor of evil. In other words, they are implying that God plans and wills everything that happens. Thankfully, that is not the case. Even if one believes God is powerful in the traditional sense of having the power to unilaterally control any outcome—but that God has chosen not to control free creatures and is bound by God's own self-binding decision—the reality remains the same: Because God is love, God doesn't control people or events, whether by volition, or due to God's uncontrolling loving nature.

Those events mentioned above can happen to any one of us, even if we are fully surrendered, God-lovers. Any view that implies God is in control of all things and can instantly change our circumstances (or keep us from future pain and suffering)—if we trust God enough—is, while comforting, simply not true.

While God is in relationship to all creatures big and small, the only thing that God is in complete control of is God's self. That's it. So, while God can always be trusted, the same cannot necessarily be said to be true of human beings. Creatures big and small, laws of regularity, and spooky quantum anomalies cannot always be trusted to have our well-being in mind. Horrific events occur because randomness, lawlike regularities, and human choices collide.

Here is the problem: If I told you that you could trust God to get what you desperately wanted or needed, and all you had to do was continue to trust and pray, I would be lying to you. The truth of our reality outweighs the consequences of the fantasy we desire. Why? First, we are invited to put away childish fantasies, to grow up, and see reality for what it is. We don't live in a Disney movie. The truth, as harsh as it can be at times, will set us free. Secondly, if people trust the finger-snapping genie God, who some preachers

MARK GREGORY KARRIS 213

and teachers suggest God is, and they do not get the things for which they trusted God, they often blame and distrust God. They feel like God has let them down, and their hearts grow cold. Some even abandon God altogether!

"Already, Mark. You are making me depressed. What is the good news then? Can we trust God for anything?"

Abso-freakin-lutely!

Whether a loved one dies by the hands of a terrorist, our limbs are cut off due to an accident, our children are killed by a sick maniac, someone we know gets sexually assaulted, or someone dies from a random rock falling off of a cliff, we can trust that God is always good, loving, and trustworthy.

"Trustworthy? How?!"

We can trust that while God won't (or can't) always give us pristine circumstances, devoid of suffering and heartache, God's loving character and commitment to shalom remains constant. We can know that a loving God does everything possible to stop evil from occurring, but simply cannot forcefully stop every terrible event from happening. We can trust that God is the smartest, wisest, most loving, and most personable agent in the room—at all times. We can trust that God is an expert of healing love, a virtuoso who is, moment-to-moment, serenading the universe through God's Spirit and captivating those who lend an ear.

We can trust that God's love is trustworthy and that it never fails. However, there is a paradox here. God's love does fail at accomplishing God's will in our lives precisely because God's love is uncontrolling. The very fact that we can "grieve the Holy Spirit" (Ephesians 4:30), shows us that God doesn't always get what God wants. However, God never fails at loving us, moment-to-moment. Just as when I go to lovingly save someone from jumping off a bridge, and they jump anyway, and it is appropriate to say, "I failed in my attempt to save them," when God is not able to achieve God's goals of increasing love, beauty, healing, and truth in our lives and in the world, God fails. God fails all the time at getting what God wants. *And*, God's love never fails.

God is good all the time, and all the time God is good. Every moment pulsates with the love of God. If my relative is sick, I can trust that God is lovingly and compassionately doing the best God can to heal them within an array of vast complexities and agencies. If we need a miracle in our lives, we can trust that God loves to show up in creative and unexpected ways while working alongside other people and creaturely elements.

Sometimes, when we fully trust and surrender our hearts to God, amazing things can happen. But there are no guarantees. The most beautiful gift that can be received, when one fully trusts God, is the peace of God that even in the midst of the storms of life—which transcends all understanding—can guard our hearts and minds in the beauty of God's perfect, moment-to-moment, uncontrolling, and co-operative love.

I understand that coming to believe that God is not in control, and that God does not dictate every action, reaction, or happening on this planet, can provide discomfort for some and emotional chaos for others. For many, believing that God is not in control is an existential slap in the face that brings an enormous amount of anxiety. There is a reason why the "God is in control of everything" theology has stuck around as long as it has. It can be quite comforting to know that we don't have to worry because God is on top of things down here. What happens is said to happen because God wants it to happen as part of God's mysterious plan. Things happen for a reason. Things are the way they are supposed to be. It all sounds good, but it just ain't so.

As you travel this D/R journey, you can trust in God's goodness. God did not desire for you to be taught hideous doctrines and for you to believe them. God did not want or allow that evil to happen to you or a loved one. I want you to know and wholeheartedly believe that.

Speaking of the phrase, "God Allowed," let's examine it. The 9/11 attack was a terrible tragedy in America's history. I was in New York at the time and was vicariously traumatized watching the terrible events unfold. How could God be thanked in the midst of such a horrific event? Many people said God shouldn't be.

They are right in their logic. If God intentionally allowed 9/11 to occur, it would be hard to be thankful toward God. Saying God allowed 9/11 suggests that God could have *dis*allowed it. Saying, "God allowed," suggests God could have stopped the evil event from happening. This, however, makes God out to be a voyeur who arbitrarily jumps into time, willfully intervening to stop some tragedies but not others. "God allows" suggests that through God's inaction, God intentionally consents to each horrific or tragic event that occurs. Is that the sort of view of God, we want to promote?

I propose that we Christians need to get rid of the phrase "God allows." If we did, I suspect fewer people would be confused about God's role or, worse, blame God for the horrific events that occur. Eliminating "God allows" could remove an unnecessary, cognitive, and emotional obstacle that prevents many from having a loving and grateful connection with their Creator.

We can trust that God is not allowing and disallowing specific forms of abuse and evil to occur. God always desires that we pray and conspire with God to thwart and eradicate injustice and evil. God is always seeking to do the miraculous. God is with you. God is for you. God can always be trusted to be, and remain, what God is: love. God's unconventional love—God's perfect, moment-to-moment, uncontrolling, and co-operative love—is captivating!

Excerpt from the book, *Religious Refugees: (De)Constructing Toward Spiritual and Emotional Healing,* by Mark Karris, Quoir Publishing, 2020

15

CONCLUSION: ALWAYS LOVED. ALWAYS FORGIVEN.

BRANDON ANDRESS

I want to share a couple of stories with you that I recently heard.

A preacher was recounting a time several years ago when, during the "invitation hymn" after the sermon, a lady came forward to be baptized. The preacher had previously heard about this lady, as he had been told that she was currently living with her boyfriend, who was already a member of the church. As they stood together in front of the congregation, the pastor reflected that he knew he "needed to confront her about her sinful relationship."

And that is exactly what he did.

As they exited to change clothes and prepare for the baptism, the preacher cornered her and said, "There is no way I can baptize you unless you quit living in sin."

The couple gave him their assurances that they wouldn't live together. The lady was baptized. And they never went back to his church again.

As if it couldn't get any worse, in the same sermon, the preacher proudly recalled a funeral he was to give to a 19-year old young man he did not know personally, but whom he soon found out was a motorcycle biker.

As the preacher was on his way to the funeral, he detailed his approach to the funeral home. He said that he saw a parking lot full of "stereotypical [bikers] with long hair and tattoos all over the place, right there in public smoking their joints and drinking [beer], with several of them having their girls along with them dressed immodestly on the back of their bikes."

As I listened to these heartbreaking words and the tone in which they were spoken, all I could think was, "Would Jesus ride passed these bikers and their 'immodestly dressed girls' in judgment based upon how they looked and then think that he needed to preach the gospel to them when they come into the funeral home?

Or, would he have gone out to them, embraced them, cried with them, listened to their stories of how they knew the young man, and then told them about the beautiful invitation and present reality of God's kingdom that surrounds them and invites them in?"

To me, the answer is so clear and so evident.

Throughout the Gospels, Jesus was always at the table of invitation with all types of people, but especially those who were regarded as outcasts and those who were stigmatized by society- tax collectors, prostitutes, the unclean, the disabled, and every type of special sin group at that time.

WHO ARE OUR GUIDES?

I wish I could tell you that stories like those above are anomalies.

But they are not.

I remember a time, as a young man, when I overheard chatter among people in my church about a lady who was wearing a mini-skirt and how she needed to be told to dress modestly in the "House of the Lord."

As soon as the service ended, an elder of the church approached the young woman, who had never been to our church before, and told her that if she was going to come back she needed to dress appropriately.

She never came back.

I share these stories for a specific reason.

The world in which we live is full of men and women from all walks of life who long for something more than what they awake to each morning. They are people we meet and cross paths with, who have their own struggles, and who know intuitively, who know down deep in their souls, that there has to be so much more to this life.

And they are just like us. People who may have had a moment in their past when heaven and earth overlapped, when they tasted something wonderful and divine, and have been desperately searching to find it again. Even if they couldn't name the experience, or really even describe it, they knew that they wanted to find it again.

But in the very place where they believed they might discover it, the church, they were instead met with judgment, expectations that they must already be perfect, and rules of perfection which they must follow.

And this is one of many reasons why so many have given up on going to church. We are hungry for so much more than what we are finding within their walls.

We are those desperately trying to make sense of this chaotic and upside-down world that feels like it is blowing up all around us. We are those attempting to make sense of faith and spirituality in a world where it looks like there is just too much suffering and too much evil prevailing. We are those searching after something of substance that we hope will lead us into more abundant lives. We are those starving and hungry for *life to the fullest*, those longing to be fully awake and fully alive, and those who want to find a greater sense of wholeness, completeness, and harmony in all things.

But who is guiding us? Who is helping us learn how to see, and then to be, differently in the world?

Religion has largely been more preoccupied with belonging systems and controlling *who's in* and *who's out* and sin management than guiding people through the wreckage, and into a more beautiful, more abundant way of living.

And it is for this reason why I am convinced that, in addition to the masses of people leaving the institutionalized church, the vast majority of visionaries and prophets are outside the walls of the church right now as well.

They are going directly to the people who are deconstructing their faith and who are still searching for something of meaning and substance, and then guiding them into the ways of *shalom*. These visionaries and prophets desperately long for churches to awaken and lead their people and their cities and towns in the ways of *shalom*, and to be instrumental in helping put the broken pieces of their communities back together. And some churches are starting to do just that. But the vast majority are presently too consumed with themselves and their own interests. And to that end, we can no longer wait on churches to figure this out.

A NEW WAY OF SPEAKING

The words of Jesus to the religious capture this tension so perfectly when he says, "You shut the door of the kingdom of [God] in people's faces. You yourselves do not enter, nor will you let those enter who are trying."[97]

Don't get lost here in the language of the kingdom of God. Jesus was speaking to people who understood kings and kingdoms and lords and it all made perfect sense to them at that time.

But that is not the way we speak any more.

97. Matthew 23:13 NIV

The kingdom of God can be understood by us as this present embrace of perfect freedom and perfect love. It is an unconditional and forgiving love that has always been present with us and has always surrounded us, enveloped us, fully immersed us, and never abandoned us. It is the present union and communion with God that transforms us, and then begins to extend outward in wholeness and completeness and harmony in all things. It is the present marriage, the present coming together, of heaven and earth in our lives.

The kingdom of God is shalom. It is the life we were always meant to live, because that is the only place where life to the fullest is found.

So with this phrase, the kingdom of God, Jesus is simply talking about a present life experience that people are searching to discover and trying to enter, but that religion blocks them from ever discovering. And surprisingly, as Jesus says, the religious haven't entered into it either. So not only have the religious not entered into this life of *shalom*, they actually keep others from discovering and entering into it.

The religious may have the very best of intentions, but this embrace, this freedom, this love does not originate *from* them, nor is it entered *through* them. It doesn't come from following the "right rules," or being on the "right religious team," or by avoiding certain "sins."

There is a parable of the kingdom of God that Jesus shares of a man who finds a treasure that had been hidden in a field. Through his own searching, he discovers the riches and then sells everything he has to buy the field in order to have all of the riches of this treasure.[98]

This short story reveals an amazing paradox and a poignant truth about our fundamental humanity and what it means to be alive. *The riches of an abundant life only come through our own searching and willingness to give up everything in order to receive what we*

98. Matthew 13:44

have discovered. It doesn't come from anyone else. It can only be discovered by you.

And that is a game changer.

It is a truth so profound and relevant today because there are many people, even within the churches, who are searching desperately for the wholeness and completeness of a better life, but who do not realize that there is actually something beyond themselves that can satisfy their every longing, that can satiate their deepest hunger, that can awaken their senses to the profound beauty around them. The sad reality, for many, is that this treasure remains hidden because they have been looking in all the wrong places and looking to all the wrong people.

Shalom is not found in a classroom, earned by religious affiliation or practice, received through the proper steps, or handed down from one person to another. It can only be found by the humble, earnest seeker who simply receives that which has been surrounding them the entire time, the *shalom* of God.

In the book *The Practice of the Presence of God*, which is a collection of writings from a 17th century monk named Brother Lawrence, he is quoted as saying, "There is no sweeter manner of living in the world than continuous communion with God. Only those who have experienced it can understand."[99]

Jesus echoes that exact sentiment when he says, "Wide is the gate and broad is the road that leads to destruction, and many enter through it. But small is the gate and narrow the road that leads to life, and only a few find it."[100]

While many wrongly ascribe those words of Jesus to a future heaven and future hell, that is not at all what he is talking about.

Jesus is talking about the difficulty of discovering the present experience of the kingdom of God. Those who have never searched for the life-giving present reality of the kingdom of God, the

---

99. Lawrence, Brother Lawrence, *His Conversations and Letters on the Practice of the Presence of God.* Cincinnati, Ohio: Forward Movement Publications, 1960. Print.

100.   Matthew 7:13-14 NIV

present life of *shalom*, will continue with lives that move toward, and further compound, destruction and wreckage. But those who continue searching will discover the narrow way, which few actually find, that leads to a sweeter manner of living in constant communion with God. Narrow is that path that leads to life and only those who seek after it will find it.

TAKING BACK BORN AGAIN

There is an absolutely fascinating encounter between Jesus and a high-ranking religious man named Nicodemus. When the religious man approaches Jesus under the cover of night, Jesus says to him, "No one can see, or experience, the *kingdom of God* unless they are born again."[101]

Please, suspend your judgment for a moment, because the phrase *born again* has been tragically hijacked by a political segment of Christianity that has given it a negative and hyper-charged meaning that was never intended. *Born again*, in the proper context, means something so much more beautiful and different than you could ever imagine.

Jesus is saying that we will never be able to *see* or *experience* this *shalom*, that we will never be able to be whole, complete, or in perfect harmony with all things in the present, unless we are born from above, unless we open ourselves in a posture of humility to actually receive this embrace of God in the Spirit.

Even more, Jesus is saying all of this to *a religious man*!

Jesus is saying that it is possible to miss the most important thing underneath the title, the position, the costume, the appearance, the weekly attendance, the revivals, the Sunday School classes, the strategic planning meetings, the offerings, and the smiles and handshakes. And to the extent we have believed any of that extraneous stuff matters to God, we have been mistaken.

101.   John 3:1-21

It is entirely possible to miss *shalom*, because no matter who you are, you will never discover what you are not actively seeking, even if you believe you are going through all the right steps. Because when religion becomes a pursuit of anything other than seeking to discover the *shalom* of God, it has completely missed the heart of God.

God's intention has only and always been intimate union. It has been for God's presence to be born within each of us. And this intimate, relational union with the Divine is the only place where *shalom* can be found. It is the only place where one can become whole, complete, and in harmony with all things.

It is also the place where each of us are on equal footing before God. It is the place where no one person is any better or worse than another. So no matter how important, how decorated, how influential, how knowledgeable, how righteous, or how powerful any single person may think they are, even if they are preachers or those in leaderships positions, *we are all in the same position together*.

And this understanding begins to help us think differently about *sin* and *forgiveness*.

But again, we are dealing with two negatively hyper-charged and powerfully loaded words that have been force fed into our collective psyche, so allow some space before jumping to any conclusions about what these words actually mean.

RETHINKING SIN

Interestingly, close to eighty-percent of the time the word *sin* is used in the New Testament, it is used as a noun.

This is interesting because we typically hear people talk about *sin* as a verb.

They describe all of the bad things we do that make God angry at us. And inevitably, when people focus on *sin* primarily as a verb, they get obsessed with saying *this sin* is worse than *that sin*. *This sin* can be overlooked but *that sin* can't. And *this sin* is unforgivable but *that sin* is okay (since we are all doing it).

The original Greek word for *sin*, as a noun, is *hamartia*. It means *to be without a share in*, or *a position where one has missed the mark or strayed*.[102]

Sin is simply a position in which we find ourselves.

It is a position out of alignment with God, or in *disunion* with God. And in that place of disunion, we are the opposite of *shalom*, the opposite of wholeness, completeness, and harmony in all things.

And this begins to open our eyes to the central issue.

It's not that we are horrible wretches for committing all of these terrible sins every day. It is that we are collectively, and equally, in a position of *disunion* with the Divine. And when we live out of this broken relationship, it very naturally begins to look unwhole, incomplete, and inharmonious. It is the natural consequence of us living outside of *shalom*.

That is why God's intention has always been to get rid of *sin*, or to remove the relational barrier between us, because we were always meant to be in *union* with God, where *life to the fullest* is found.

The wisdom of Paul ought to be an eye-opener for each one of us today, because he echoes this exact point when he says that we all fall short of God's glory.[103] We are all in the same position of disunion, equally. There is not one single person who has a position that is any better or any worse than another. And in this position, we are not presently sharing in this *shalom*.

That is sin, as a noun.

So when religious people begin creating these crazy hierarchies of *sin* and telling us that certain people or groups are worse than others, telling us *who's in* and *who's out*, all it does is alienate and devalue people who should not be alienated or devalued. It sends a message that the religious are good and righteous and all the rest of us are sinners who are bad and unworthy. And all that does is create more judgment and condemnation and anger and hostility toward people, which leads to more walls of division between us all.

---

102.   Gary Hill, *HELPS Word Studies*.

103.   Romans 3:23

The point is that when the religious view *sin* primarily, or exclusively, as a verb, they fall back into that old way of labeling, categorizing, ranking, and then dividing. And it completely misses the big picture that we are all in the same position and that the heart of God has always been an invitation back into relational union with every single one of us equally.

Every. Single. One. Of. Us. Equally.

So when we begin to see *sin* correctly, as a place of disunion, we understand there can be no hierarchy of sin or worthiness. We are all disconnected from the Source of Life, and we are in that place together.

Hard stop.

And once we begin to understand this simple truth, it is the place where humility and grace comes to life and shines. It is the place of remarkable beauty and breakthrough. It is the place where all the broken pieces of the world come back together as one, where we learn how to see beauty in the wreckage, and where everyone is welcome to the table of invitation together, without judgment or exclusion, whether you are living with someone, a biker who drinks beer and smokes a little weed, or a young lady wearing a short skirt.

I AM SO SORRY

If this truth has been withheld from you, or if you have received something very different than this message of radical invitation and inclusion, please let me tell you that the grace and love of God has always been with you, has always been for you, and has always surrounded you. The grace and love of God has always been with you, even in your disunion, even when you have felt unworthy, and has always been inviting you back with open arms, as you are, into loving union with the Source of Life.

But there may be some of you, maybe a lot of you, who are reading these words and still carrying around so much pain and so many wounds from past church experiences or past dealings with religious people.

I am deeply sorry and I completely understand.

But.

No matter what you may have been told.

No matter how badly you may have been treated or wounded.

No matter the judgments and accusations that may have been thrown at you.

No matter if you may have been told that you are unworthy or unredeemable.

No matter if you may have been told that God will never forgive you.

Let me tell you emphatically, once and for all, that you are loved and you are already forgiven, as you are.

Every single one of you.

Forgiven.

Past tense.

Done deal.

God loves you and has always been inviting you, as you are, into *shalom*. Inviting you, as you are, out of the wreckage and into a new beginning of life and love and beauty and wholeness and completeness and harmony. Inviting you, as you are, into the full immersion of an entirely different present reality. And God is speaking your name to let you know that you have always been loved as you are, that you have always been worthy as you are, and that in this embrace of the Divine you are being made whole.

I rarely say this, but when I do you know I mean it. Praise God!

RETHINKING THE FORGIVENESS OF GOD

Let's talk about forgiveness. You may have always thought of forgiveness as a verbal sentiment only given when an adequate measure of contrition, remorse, or tears have been poured out. And that is completely understandable, because that is the model of forgiveness we have been culturally-conditioned to understand, especially in our churches. Within that model, forgiveness is conditionally given in exchange for a person being sorry for their sins. The key word is *conditionally*.

It usually plays out something like this. God has the power to forgive you or to not forgive you. And God's forgiveness will absolutely not be given unless you are really sorry for what you have done and then go through all the right steps to show how sorry you are.

But interestingly, what we find in Scripture is actually something very different than the conditional, reactive forgiveness that holds power over people.

In story after story, and account after account, we discover that the forgiveness of God, demonstrated through the life and teachings of Jesus, is *unconditional* and *preemptive*. It happens before any of us acknowledge it or do anything to receive it.

God's forgiveness is always unmerited and given before anyone ever asks for it.

There is absolutely nothing anyone can do to earn that kind of forgiveness, because it is birthed out of compassion and mercy and is given regardless of one being sorry.

But many miss God's unconditional, preemptive forgiveness because they project their merit-based forgiveness system on to God and then look at the Bible as a mechanical process to be exactly followed or as a mathematical equation that only equals forgiveness if all of the numbers are added up correctly.

The forgiveness of God is not based upon merit and is neither a mechanical process to follow, nor a mathematical equation to get correct, in order to receive it.

God's forgiveness is completely a one-sided and was demonstrated at the cross of Christ for all people, for all time. In every way the religious have believed, or continue to believe, that non-stop sacrifices, penance, or daily words of contrition are necessary on our part to be at peace with an angry, temperamental god, it was God who finally put those faulty assumptions to rest, once and for all, by offering a peace sacrifice *to us*, not continually expecting sacrifices *from us*.

Stop and think about that for a moment.

It was God that made a peace offering to us, in Jesus, to prove that there is absolutely no hostility or anger toward us. There is only a longing to be at peace with us and then to be in relationship with us. And in any way we have rebelled from that peace and relationship, it has already been forgiven.

So rather than an authoritarian power play that holds forgiveness or unforgiveness over our heads until we are contrite and remorseful enough, or until we have offered enough sacrifices, or until we have shed enough tears, the forgiveness of God stands alone. It has never been dependent upon any single person climbing the ladder of worthiness or attaining higher levels on the fictitious relative sin scale. It is unconditionally and preemptively self-giving and self-generative, and birthed out of God's great compassion and mercy *for all of us*.

And as a result, there is only and always forgiveness for all equally and the hope of a restored relationship.

A MOVEMENT TOWARD RELATIONSHIP

God's forgiveness has always been God's first move toward restoring a relationship with each of us. And if you have missed that then you have missed the entire point.

The forgiveness of God allows for the repairing and mending work in our relationship to begin. For the two to become one. For that which has been divided to come back together. For that which has been in disunion to be reunited. For wholeness, completeness, and harmony to be realized in our relationship. That is precisely what reconciliation is. It is the process that slowly begins to build trust, heal wounds and divisions, and make relationships whole again over time.

And that is the hope of God. That in light of God's forgiveness, our relationship will be reconciled, will be made whole and complete, will move toward perfect harmony, and *shalom* will be realized in and through our lives.

Interestingly, that is why followers of Jesus are referred to as *ministers of reconciliation*, rather than *ministers of forgiveness*.[104] Because God's forgiveness has already been given to all. That is the Good News. And now, in light of God's forgiveness for all people, we are those who announce to the world that there is no enmity, hostility, or condemnation from God toward anyone. There is only love and forgiveness and open arms that welcomes back every prodigal.

BREAKING INTO WHAT IS ALREADY THERE

I want to share something very eye opening and mind-blowing with you.

On the day of Pentecost, Peter is preaching to the crowd and says, "Repent and be baptized, every one of you, in the name of Jesus Christ *for* the forgiveness of your sins."

From the outside looking in, it sounds like Peter is telling the people that in order to be forgiven, they must first repent and be baptized and then, and only then, will they be forgiven by God.

And that is the way countless Christians have taken that verse over the centuries. It is viewed as a conditional transaction between God and a person. In essence, the forgiveness of God will only be given *when* you say the right words, when you have a repentant heart, and when you are baptized in the water.

But here is the crazy part.

In that verse spoken by Peter, the word translated as *for* is the Greek word *eis*.

Eis means *a motion into, penetration, union*.[105]

So what many have always read as this conditional transaction between people and God is actually a movement we make into something that is already there, something that has already been given, something that already surrounds us. And that something... is the forgiveness of God.

---

104.   2 Corinthians 5: 11-21

105.   Gary Hill, *HELPS Word Studies*.

We don't do something for God's forgiveness. We move into, and find union with, a forgiveness that already surrounds us.

And our faithful acts of repentance and baptism are those movements we make that penetrate into, and find union with, that forgiveness that was given long ago.

God's forgiveness is not being withheld like a stingy miser. Nor is it dependent upon you being good or perfect, or going through the right steps. God's forgiveness is already here. It has already been extended to all. It is all around you. The invitation into forgiveness and a life of *shalom* was given long ago. All you have to do is enter into it.

And no one can keep you from entering, as you are.

WHY DOES THIS MATTER?

The reason this matters is because we ultimately extend that which we believe has been extended to us. And as long as we believe that God only forgives those who ask for it, those who deserve it, and those who are repentant, then we will do the same with others.

This is single-handedly the most important reason for us to understand that God's forgiveness is unconditional and preemptive, because it truly affects how we view and treat other people.

For instance, if my sister was sideways with my dad, but my dad already unconditionally and preemptively forgave her, what right would I have in continuing to finger point, accuse, and hold it against my sister?

Since my father had already forgiven her, ought it not change how I see my sister (as forgiven)? Ought it not open my eyes to see how I am not in a position to accuse, condemn, or be hostile toward her? Ought it not cause me to be as forgiving toward her as my father?

Understanding God's forgiveness is not a matter of subtle nuance or simply a chicken and egg discussion without any real world practical consequence. This distinction matters so much right now.

It matters for how Christians view and then treat other people, especially the LGBTQ community, drug addicts and abusers, the homeless, those who are in our country illegally, and any other group that is being judged and marginalized.

IT'S SO GOOD TO BE ALIVE

To be really blunt here, it has never been more important than it is today to abandon self-limiting, self-assured religion and discover life in the *shalom* of God.

Because when we are immersed into the radical forgiveness and inclusion of the Divine, we are surrounded by the very heart of God, which has always been an unconditional, self-sacrificing, other-centered love. And when we penetrate head-first into the forgiveness and lovingkindness of God, we begin to change at the heart level and it changes how we see other people and how we experience this life in all of its brilliance and fullness. In this intimate, relational union with God, we actually begin to become like our Father.

God's unconditional love becomes our unconditional love.

So what you may have never tasted in the past, or what you may have only tasted in part for a fleeting moment in the past, has now become a life overflowing in abundance in this present moment.

But this time.

It's here with us in every present moment moving forward. Heaven birthed within us, no longer as fleeting, transient moments that slip through our fingers, but as our new way of living, as a newborn, as a new creation, as a little child, with new eyes, a new heart, and breathing as if for the very first time.

It is so good to be alive again. And this is what God wants for us all.

But unless we become like little children, unless we are born again, unless we seek after and discover this new reality, we will never see or experience the kingdom of God in this life. We will never discover anything outside the limitations of religion. We will never move beyond our disunion with the Divine, nor enter into the present union of *shalom*.

But when we do, we carry this new life with us into every experience. This peace and forgiveness within our souls begins to flow into our every interaction and conversation and relationship. This joy in our being begins to delight in the resident goodness of all things- every sight, every sound, every touch, and every scent. And this deep love in our hearts begins to awaken us to a beauty in all things that we may have previously missed or taken for granted.

Like sitting in silence and meditating and praying and communing in the life-giving presence of God. Taking an early morning walk and contemplating the beauty of creation and giving thanks for all that we awake to every morning. Sitting down for a meal with our families and friends each evening after a long day. Seeing every person as a brother or sister who is unconditionally loved. Hugging the brokenhearted, sharing words of life and encouragement to those who are having a hard time, or making a meal for the family who lost a loved one. Serving meals and sitting at a table in conversation with those who gather at the hot meal site. Visiting and caring for the widow in our neighborhoods. Holding the hand of our spouse during their chemotherapy treatment. Remembering all of those moments in our lives and cherishing them and giving thanks for it all.

It's every single moment of our lives, even in the hardship, even in the pain, even in the wreckage where heaven and earth come together, where a new reality births within us and we begin to see and experience all things differently.

And that is so much more than religion could ever give you.

Excerpt from the book, *Beauty In The Wreckage: Finding Peace in the Age of Outrage*, by Brandon Andress, Quoir Publishing, 2018.

ADDITIONAL RESOURCES

Let's keep the conversation going. Many of the contributors and authors in the book are connecting to others and sharing what they've learned so far on these platforms. Please consider joining us. We'd love to connect with you and learn more about your journey.

ONLINE COMMUNITY

- **Heresy After Hours Facebook Group**

  Heresy After Hours exists to provide a safe place for those undergoing religious deconstruction (especially from conservative evangelical Christian backgrounds). We aim to have conversations as well as share ideas and resources that many Christians might consider …. heretical. The goal here is to provide a safe space, nothing more and nothing less. We tend to be equal parts healthy vulnerability and witty sarcasm to help deconstruct the journey. Join us at www.facebook.com/groups/heresyafterhours/

ONLINE COURSES

- **Square 1**

  Deconstruction isn't easy. But you don't need to go through it alone. *Square 1* is a 12-week online course and community devoted to helping you navigate the Deconstruction/Reconstruction process. Here's what some of our students have to say about their experiences in *Square 1:*

  - *"You have no idea how much I love this [Square 1] group and how much I look forward to our weekly sessions."* – Mike Craig

  - *"For me, Square 1 has been a safe space where I have been lovingly encouraged to work through these questions—and better still have been the questions of others in our group. Please don't give up on God, or get stuck in bitterness and pain without doing this course first. I have started to learn how to love again."* – Kenneth Fleck

  - *"Lots to digest! And so, so good! This session alone has been worth the money and time invested. Excited to talk this one through with everyone on our call. Be there, or be square (pun intended)."* – Diane Nichols

  Special 75% discount offer: Use the coupon code **B4ULOSE75** when you register to receive this massive discount. You can learn more and register for Square 1 at: www.BK2SQ1.com.

PODCASTS

- **Heretic Happy Hour**

  Burning questions. Not people. Co-hosted by Keith Giles, Matthew Distefano, Rev. Dr. Katy Valentine, and Derrick Day. Visit www.HereticHappyHour.com

- **The Messy Spirituality Podcast**

  The Messy Spirituality Podcast is all about finding God in unexpected places. Visit www.MessySpirituality.org

- **Book Ish: The Canon Continues**

  The podcast that's dismantling the sacred/secular divide book by book. Visit www.BookIsh.cc

- **The Bonfire Sessions**

  With rawness and vulnerability, as well as a large dose of salty language, the hosts of The Bonfire Sessions spend one night a week around a fire pit, chatting about the big ideas of life. Sometimes funny, sometimes profound, but always honest, the two hosts will be sure to challenge your heart, soul, and mind. Visit www.TheBonfireSessions.net

BOOKS

- *Jesus Untangled: Crucifying Our Politics To Pledge Allegiance To The Lamb* by Keith Giles

- *Jesus Unbound: Liberating The Word Of God From The Bible* by Keith Giles

- *Jesus Unveiled: Forsaking Church As We Know It For Ekklesia As God Intended* by Keith Giles

- *Jesus Undefeated: Condemning The False Doctrine Of Eternal Torment* by Keith Giles

- *Jesus Unexpected: Ending The End Times To Become The Second Coming* by Keith Giles

- *Jesus Unforsaken: Substituting Divine Wrath With Unrelenting Love* by Keith Giles

- *Beauty In The Wreckage: Finding Peace in the Age of Outrage* by Brandon Andress

- *Into The Gray: The Mental and Emotional Aftermath of Spiritual Deconstruction* by Michelle Collins

- *Deconstructing Religion* by Derrick Day

- *Heretic!: An LGBTQ-Affirming, Divine Violence-Denying, Christian Universalist's Responses to Some of Evangelical Christianity's Most Pressing Concerns* by Matthew J. Distefano

- *From the Blood of Abel: Humanity's Root Causes of Violence and the Bible's Theological-Anthropological Solution* by Matthew J. Distefano

- *All Set Free: How God is Revealed in Jesus and Why That is Really Good News* by Matthew J. Distefano

- *The Wages of Grace: A Novel* by Brandon Dragan

- *Religious Refugees: (De)Constructing Toward Spiritual and Emotional Healing* by Mark Gregory Karris

- *Divine Echoes: Reconciling Prayer With the Uncontrolling Love of God* by Mark Gregory Karris

- *Saying No To God: A Radical Approach to Reading the Bible Faithfully* by Matthew J. Korpman

- *Shame: An Unconventional Memoir* by Josh Roggie

- *For You Were Bought with a Price: Sex, Slavery, and Self-Control in a Pauline Community* by Rev. Dr. Katy Valentine

- *Take Nothing With You: Rethinking the Role of Missionaries* by Skeeter Wilson

AUTHOR BIOGRAPHIES

BRANDON ANDRESS

Brandon is the author of bestselling *Beauty in the Wreckage: Finding Peace in the Age of Outrage*. As a freelance writer, he has contributed his work to Relevant Magazine, ReKnew, and Zondervan. Brandon lives in Columbus, Indiana and is a graduate of Hanover College in Psychology with an MBA from Indiana Wesleyan University.

MICHELLE COLLINS

Michelle is the author of *Into the Gray, the Mental and Emotional Aftermath of Spiritual Deconstruction*. She holds multiple degrees in business and theology culminating in her latest venture of a doctorate in psychology. In addition to the scholastic endeavors, Michelle is a competing bodybuilder, business owner, and mother to 4 grown children. She currently lives in Murfreesboro Tennessee and is adjusting to seasons once again.

DERRICK DAY

Derrick Day is a dynamic speaker, teacher, author, and leadership coach. He is a 30-plus year veteran of Information Technology (IT) consulting and management. Derrick has also been a newspaper columnist with the New Journal and Guide and a former radio talk-show host with WNIS-AM in Norfolk, Virginia. He is also a seven-year veteran of the United States Navy. He is the author of *Deconstructing Religion* (available on amazon.com and createspace.com) and is currently working on several other fiction and non-fiction books. Derrick is also the founder and former Pastor of Agape Dominion Outreach and Founder and Bishop of Kingdom Covenant International, a ministry governance organization. He also the Former President and Presiding Bishop of the International Circle of Faith (ICOF) and is former General Secretary of Kingdom Builders Association of America. Derrick's personal mission is demonstrating how Love transforms and impacts every area of life—including relationships, business, education, and government. Derrick is married to author Angela Day and they are the proud parents of five sons.

BRANDON DRAGAN

Brandon Dragan grew up in New Jersey, a stone's throw from the Lincoln Tunnel. At eighteen he left home to pursue his dreams in Nashville, Tennessee. He is currently a 2L Juris Doctor candidate at Belmont University College of Law. Brandon and his wife Jami live in the Nashville area with their two daughters, Natalie and Brooklyn. He enjoys a good cigar, Irish whisky, road cycling, and is an avid supporter of Arsenal Football Club. Connect with him at www.BrandonDragan.com

MATTHEW DISTEFANO

Matthew J. Distefano is the author of multiple books, cohost of the *Heretic Happy Hour* podcast, a long-time social worker, and hip-hop artist. You can find his work at www.AllSetFree.com

JASON ELAM

Jason Elam is Brandi's grateful husband, proud dad of 4 awesome kids, a former professional wrestler and radio broadcaster, and former local church pastor for over 20 years. Jason is the creator of *The Messy Spirituality Podcast* and a contributor for Patheos. You can connect with Jason on Facebook, Twitter, and Instagram.

MARIA FRANCESCA FRENCH

Maria currently is Director and Creator of H&Co., working towards theological innovation and imagination, informed by asking new questions of God, community, faith and church, after a 10-year tenure of working with theological schools that. She holds a Master of Arts in Religion and Theology as well a Master of Arts in Christian Thought. Maria has also spent time pursuing research interests with London School of Theology that include Philosophical Hermeneutics and Continental Philosophy. She is currently engaged in Doctoral work with Wesley Theological Seminary in the Cambridge track studying the intersection of faith, theology and culture in a world where the philosophical landscape is ever changing. As a teacher of things Christian and Post Christian, Radical Theology and Post-Theist thinker, a purveyor of story and faith futurist, Maria is passionate about moving into the future with a contextual faith that matters. Maria has gone from native New Yorker to transplant Minnesotan to living in the South of France and has recently moved from SoCal to the UK, as she has recently married and settled there with her British husband. www.MariaFrancescaFrench.com

KEITH GILES

Keith Giles is a former pastor who abandoned the pulpit to follow Jesus and ended up founding a church where 100% of the offering is given away to help the poor in the community. He is the author of the best-selling "Jesus Un" book series, including *Jesus Untangled, Jesus Unbound, Jesus Unveiled, Jesus Undefeated, Jesus Unexpected* and *Jesus Unforsaken*. Keith is the co-host of the *Heretic Happy Hour* podcast and blogs regularly on Patheos at www.KeithGiles. com .He has appeared on CNN, USA Today, BuzzFeed, and John Fugelsang's "Tell Me Everything." Keith and his wife, Wendy, recently moved to El Paso, TX to embark on their next adventure with *Peace Catalyst International.*

MARK KARRIS

Mark Gregory Karris is an adjunct professor at Point Loma Nazarene University, a licensed marriage and family therapist in private practice in San Diego, California, an ordained pastor, husband, and recording artist. He's a voracious reader, researcher and all around biophilic. He has received a master's degree in counseling through the Alliance Graduate School of Counseling in Nyack, N.Y., a master of divinity from Drew Theological School in N.J., and earned his Doctorate in Psychology with an emphasis in Couple and Family Therapy from Alliant International University in San Diego, CA. Mark is the author of the best-selling books *Religious Refugees: (De)Constructing Toward Spiritual and Emotional Healing* and *Divine Echoes: Reconciling Prayer with the Uncontrolling Love of God* (Quoir, 2018). You can find out more about Mark here: www.MarkGregoryKarris.com

MATTHEW J. KORPMAN

Matthew J. Korpman (PhDc in New Testament, University of Birmingham) is an adjunct professor of biblical studies at La Sierra University. He is a graduate of Yale Divinity School (MAR, Second

Temple Judaism) and holds four undergraduate degrees, including a BA in Philosophy. He is the author of the popular theological work *Saying No to God* (Quoir, 2019).

JOSH ROGGIE

Josh Roggie has been writing since his teenage years when he had aspirations of being a Christian rapper. He has long since released that dream and focused on honing his writing craft to develop stories of all kinds that would inspire challenging questions. He lives in Colorado Springs with his wife and two cats.

REV. DR. KATY VALENTINE

Katy E. Valentine is the founder of *The Metaphysical Christian*, a Facebook group of over 6,000 members, all exploring questions about metaphysics and being a Jesus follower. She is an ordained pastor and New Testament scholar, and is jazzed about justice and all of the spiritual realities that mainstream Christianity avoids like the plague. Katy also co-hosts the *Heretic Happy Hour* podcast. Also, she plays the harp.

SKEETER WILSON

Skeeter Wilson was born in Kenya, along the edge of the Gikuyu highlands, during the last years of colonialism. The son of American missionaries, he witnessed Kenya's birth pangs as it gained a semblance of independence. He spent his formative years divided between his Gikuyu friends and the children of missionaries at an American-curriculum boarding school.

Wilson earned his postgraduate African History and Creative Writing degrees while doing field research in the highlands of Kenya. His published works include Worthless People, Crossing Rivers, and Escape from Stupid. He has published short stories in several traditional and online magazines.

Take Nothing With You (Quoir, 2020) is Wilson's debut nonfiction work.

Wilson now lives in Auburn, Washington, with his wife Jacque. Together they host guests in their treehouse, put on small writers conferences, and host an annual event called the Goat N' Guzzle, which focuses on cuisine from various cultures in Africa.

Many voices. One message.

Quoir is a boutique publisher
with a singular message: *Christ is all.*
Venture beyond your boundaries to discover Christ
in ways you never thought possible.

For more information, please visit
www.quoir.com